MARTIN BUBER

PERSONALIST & PROPHET

MARTIN BUBER

Personalist & Prophet

by

DR. M. A. BEEK AND DR. J. SPERNA WEILAND

*Professors at the University
of Amsterdam*

NEWMAN PRESS

Westminster, Md. Glen Rock, N. J. New York, N. Y.

Amsterdam Toronto Montreal

Contents

Contents

Foreword

Martin Buber's work has attracted a great deal of attention in Europe and America. His influence in the fields of biblical scholarship, theology and philosophy cannot be overestimated. Many of Buber's writings have been translated into Dutch, and their influence is discussed in The Netherlands in various books and articles. However, there is still no concise survey incorporating recent literature, and that is why we have set out to write a lucid introduction to Buber's work in all its sweep and variety.

Because the area covered by Buber's activity is so large, the present authors have divided the task between them. We were aware that there is an evident and integral connection between Buber's translation and interpretation of the Old Testament, his understanding of Chassidism and his insights in the field of the philosophy of religion. A strong, animated personality lies behind all this work which, however varied in its forms of expression, is undergirded by the same basic principles.

Chapters two to five are the work of the first contributor, the rest of the second. We believe that we are sufficiently akin in mind and outlook to have avoided inconsistencies in what we have written. We have also avoided treading the same ground. In parceling out the subjects to be treated, we have borne in mind the particular academic fields in which our respective interests and knowledge lie.

We have not aimed at an exhaustive treatment. Our purpose was only to do justice to the principal themes in Buber's work over a lifetime, and we have tried to envisage what would be of most relevance and concern to our readers. We have kept in mind those many people who at this juncture are searching for a justifiable view of life and the world, and we started from the conviction that Martin Buber's wisdom does indeed help us to find a direction.

We are grateful to Miss C. Quené, assistant in the Theological
Faculty of Amsterdam University, for checking the proofs and
compiling the bibliography.

M. A. Beek
J. Sperna Weiland

Something about Martin Buber's Life

Martin Buber was born in the winter of 1878 in Vienna, capital city of the Hapsburg monarchy. Emperor Franz Joseph ruled over a kingdom that extended into Poland and Russia and far into the Balkans and was peopled with Germans and Czechs, Poles and Magyars, Croats and Serbs, and a large Jewish community concentrated in the capital and in the Polish-Russian border territories. Johann Strauss, king of the waltz, was still the rage in Vienna, the noble façade which Vienna now presents was still being built, and power in the Balkans was still being augmented in 1878 by the occupation of Bosnia and Hertzegovina, but already the monarchy was starting to disintegrate.

Martin Buber did not live in Vienna for long. He was three when his parents separated, and the child was entrusted to the care of his grandparents. They lived in Lemberg in Galicia, which up to 1918 was part of the Hapsburg Empire and was then annexed to Poland. The grandfather, Salomon Buber, was a banker and *Handelskammerrat* (a word not readily translatable) and at the same time a considerable scholar, well versed in Midrash and Jewish tradition. Martin Buber dedicated his first book to him as "the last master of the ancient Haskala." The Haskala is the Enlightenment, a putting of one's confidence in reason, and so forth, but in this Jewish milieu the Enlightenment itself bears a distinctively Jewish stamp.

It was not only the Haskala that Martin Buber encountered in Galicia. During the summer months spent in the Bukovina, in the neighborhood of the small towns of Sadagora and Czortkov, he came in contact with Chassidism. Here Israel van Rizin (d. 1850) and other *tsaddikim* were still a living memory, and here too his son, David Mosche—whom Buber did not meet—lived until 1903. But for the time being neither the Haskala nor Chassidism were to be of decisive importance to Martin Buber.

In one of his books he relates how as a child of fourteen he felt

1

constrained to delve into questions regarding space and time. Has time a beginning and an end, or is it infinite? Are there boundaries to space, or is space unlimited? The one is equally as impossible as the other—and just as unimaginable. Buber says that these questions gave him no respite and that they brought him to the edge of madness—until at fifteen years of age he found release in Kant's *prolegomena zu einer jeden künftigen Metaphysik, die als Wissenschaft wird auftreten können* (prolegomena to any future metaphysics that is to qualify as being knowledge). Two years later Nietzsche captivated him with *Also sprach Zarathustra* (*Thus Spoke Zoroaster*).

No wonder that his studies, begun in Vienna in 1896, were devoted to philosophy. In the Viennese culture of that time Buber felt very much at home. In it German, Jewish and Slav elements met and crossed with one another. Being cast in a Romantic mold, it pinned its faith more on "intuition" than on clear thinking, and it was "aesthetic" in the sense in which Kierkegaard employed that word (read, for instance, the earliest poems of Hofmannsthal and Rilke). Yet it was—as he looked back upon it—also *'olam ha-tohu*, a period and a world of chaos and confusion: the world so concisely depicted in Genesis 1, 2. But very soon he set out on another tack.

Here Nietzsche's name turns up again. In *Das Problem des Menschen*—a book that appeared in Hebrew in 1943 and was translated into German after the war—Buber writes that after Pascal and Kierkegaard, Nietzsche has posed the question of man with unrivaled power and keenness. No doubt Nietzsche is a romantic too, but his language is sterner, his thinking sharper and more engaged than anything Buber encountered in Vienna. And though Buber says later on that "everything in Nietzsche's ruminations that is meant to afford an answer [to the question of man] is beside the point," there can be no doubt that Nietzsche made a great impression on him. The remarkable thing is that the fact of his being a Jew is so little in evidence during this period. There is reason to think that it did not mean much to him, either. Yet it was in Jewish tradition—and specifically in Chassidism—that he was to find the light that ascended over the *'olam ha-tohu*.

As was usual at the time, Buber made the rounds of the German universities. In the winter of 1897 he was in Leipzig, in the summer of '98 in Berlin, in the winter of '98-'99 back in Leipzig, in the summer of 1899 in Basle and Zurich, and in the autumn of that year again in Berlin, where he sat at the feet of Georg Simmel and Wilhelm Dilthey. He had already met Herzl in 1898, and it was after this encounter that Buber was gripped by the idea of Zionism—something that he felt to be an *Aufschwung,* a kind of "outward bound" adventure on the open sea.

At the third annual Zionist Congress held in Basle in the summer of 1898, he took the floor, declaring among other things that Zionism is not the cause of any party or faction, but a world vision and outlook needing to be enlarged and extended on all fronts. One of its essentials is a concern for Jewish culture, another the nurture of the Jewish people. For Zionism is really about new people engaged in building a new community. The "internal agitation" is all in the service of that vision. Anyone with a keen ear can already detect here something of the controversies that were to arise in the Zionist movement later on. Greater things are at stake here than the question of a Jewish State. Many years afterward he said:

> Just as where my existence *qua* human being is concerned the State does not enter into it, so where my being a Jew is concerned the Jewish State does not come into it either. And when Cohen talks about the urge to power in a people that can contrive to maintain its living identity, this means nothing to me. I have seen and heard too much of the effects of an unrestrained desire for power. The real issue is of a different kind. It is not a question of the Jewish State. If that should come into being now, it would be built, surely, on the same foundations that every modern State is built on. . . . What is really at issue is an "establishment" that independently of what moves and activates nations . . . can unite all our energies in the endeavor to build up Jewry and to make it a reality.

The position of reserve with regard to the State of Israel is already expressed here, the ideal of the kibbutz is sharply formulated, the theme enunciated that is to be worked out in *Pfade in Utopia.* The vital thing is to "restructure" the community whose structure has been lost during the era of capitalism. Power and the State, freedom and the community, humanity itself—from now on these are the major permanent motifs in Buber's thinking.

And the time is not far off when Buber is to be censured for a lack of realism.

It is in line with the way things were going that he should have been drawn to socialism and a few years later become involved in the movement known as *Die neue Gemeinschaft,* one of whose leaders was the Jewish socialist, Gustav Landauer. Later on, in *Pfade in Utopia,* Buber was to write with great affection of Landauer. Yet *Die neue Gemeinschaft*—romantic, optimistic and indeed unrealistic as it was—proved to be no more than an interlude. In 1903 Landauer left it, and not long afterward Buber followed him.

What persisted was his work for Zionism—that is, for the building up and cultural development of the Jewish movement still in its infancy in Western Europe. It was this that in the winter of 1900-01 brought him to Berlin, and the following winter to Vienna, and it was for this that in 1902, along with a number of friends, he founded the *Jüdische Verlag,* which in the autumn of that year produced the Jewish almanac and a book on Jewish artists. It was also the year in which Herzl brought out his novel about the future, *Altneuland.* But in the meantime, at the fifth Zionist Congress held in Basle toward the end of 1901, there came a rift between Herzl and his following—"political" Zionism —and the people centered around Chaim Weizmann, Martin Buber and others. For Herzl Zionism was a political movement, with the creation of a Jewish State—preferably in Palestine, although Argentina was also considered a possibility—as its goal, whereas for Buber it was above all a cultural movement, and its purpose the inner renewal of the Jewish people. The rift meant that for the time being Buber withdrew from the Zionist movement.

The years that followed were given chiefly to study—study of Chassidism, sagas and legends, and mysticism. As a result, a number of books appeared: in 1906 *Die Geschichten des Rabbi Nachman;* in 1908 *Die Legende des Baalschem;* in 1909 *Ekstatische Konfessionen;* in 1913 the remarkable and little known *Daniel: Gespräche von der Verwirklichung,* a balance of the insights that Buber had acquired from his study of mysticism, Chassidism and Chinese philosophy.

Meanwhile he had made fresh contacts with the Zionist movement, which after Herzl's death in 1904 had undergone some fairly drastic changes. There was now room for Buber and for what he had at heart. People were thinking in terms of a German-Jewish movement of renewal, which was not, however, to be confined to Jews but was to embrace humanity, Jews and Christians, Germans, Frenchmen and so on. The year was 1913. In the summer of 1914 there was a gathering at Potsdam. Martin Buber was there with Gustav Landauer and many major figures of the time. Romain Rolland was unable to attend, but Frederik van Eeden and Henri Borel were there. Sympathy for the enterprise was expressed by Walter von Rathenau. Once again the center of concern was a new type of community. A few weeks later the heir to the throne of Austria was assassinated in the Bosnian capital, and Europe was plunged into World War I.

During the war period Buber continued with his work in the Zionist movement. But Herzl was not yet forgotten, and the old controversy between political and cultural Zionism (this is of course a very graphic way of putting it) burst into life again. Once more Buber made a stand against those who were dreaming of a Jewish State:

> I would simply say this: that the idea of a Jewish State, with flag and cannon and so forth, I will have nothing to do with—not even in my dreams. How things turn out will depend on what people make of them; therefore those who are concerned about the person and about humanity must give themselves to the task—here, now that once again it lies with men to build a community, a fellowship.

That is how Buber wrote in 1918 to Stefan Zweig, and he added that he would rather take a chance on a run of tragic setbacks and disappointments than back the degeneration that would inevitably ensue from a Jewish State with its cannon, its flag and so forth. He expressed himself even more sharply in an address delivered in 1918, in which he dismissed the accusation that he and his comrades-in-arms, who were inspired by the work of Achad-Haäm, had "accommodated" themselves to the existing situation:

> It is not those who would have us serve the true God in a strange land, but you who are the conformists—you who for the

land's sake are prepared to enter the service of false gods, provided that they are called by some Jewish name. It is you who
are accommodated to the great dogma of the century. . . . Every
nation (so it is said) is its own master and its own judge,
answerable to itself alone. What it does to its own advantage is
well done; what it champions as *its* cause is a good cause.

Against that dogma, to which even many Zionists had become
enslaved, Buber set his face. On this point he had to stick to his
guns; on this point compromise was not possible. Of course, the
people, the nation, is a fundamental reality, but the nation is not
the State!

Our voice calls the Jewish people . . . to be always loyal to the
Spirit and not to revert to dogma. That will not be easy for our
nation; nor do we wish to make it easy for them. We do not
want to leave them to their own devices—that is something their
true and rightful leaders have never done. But when those leaders inquired what way had to be taken, they did not look for
counsel to the disposition of the people, but only to the Spirit
who was revealed to them and in them. And it must always be
so. Our desire is to obey the Spirit so that he may become real
through us. As long as we are of the Spirit, we have the seed of
true life within us. If the day should come when we were like all
peoples, we would no longer deserve to exist. . . .

The way is clear, then: settlement in Palestine—"revolutionary
colonization," of course—but no establishment of a Jewish State.
Such a vision is of a kindred spirit with that of *Hapul Hazair*
(The Young Worker), a group of young agricultural workers in
Palestine whose aim was colonization on a basis of socialism.
What they and their leader, A. C. Gordon, had in view was a
living community, a fellowship, which would look to the spiritual
renewal of the individual for the nation's redemption, in the direction of its "will-to-be". Buber identified himself with them
but remained in Europe, where at the twelfth Congress of the
Zionist movement, held in Carlsbad in 1921, he expounded the
ideal of "The Young Worker". This address raised for the first
time the question of the relation of the Jewish settlements in
Palestine to the Arab population. It was the period when the first
Jewish colonizers were entering Palestine, and Buber saw their
relations with the Palestinian Arabs as a crucial test of the "au-

thenticity" of what was happening there. A brainchild of his, a few years later, was the Brith Shalom association, the purpose of which was to achieve "equal co-existence" between Jews and Arabs in Palestine. But this was a vision that extended beyond Palestine to embrace the world and the whole of mankind. It was not just in the old country but everywhere that a spirit of renewal must prevail among men and nations. In 1921, that spirit led to the establishment of the *Jüdische Gesellschaft für Internationale Verständigung*. In regard to the program of this organization, Buber says, among other things:

> The situation in which we find ourselves, the situation of a war in which every man's hand is against his neighbor—whether that war be waged, as now, openly, or in secret—cannot be "abolished"; it cannot be replaced by something negative, by a state of non-war; it cannot be surmounted by anything of a formal character, by an agreement between States; only an ideal which answers to the facts and is supported by a religious conviction can bring that about.

One essential condition was the inward renewal of every people, and so the *Jüdische Gesellschaft für Internationale Verständigung* made it its aim to educate the Jewish people to perceive this condition and to realize it in their own life and conduct. The relationship between Jew and Arab in Palestine came to have an exemplary function in this context. Men must be able to see there what *menschheitliches Völkerleben* is. If it succeeded there, it could do so elsewhere; if it did not. . . .

In 1923 appeared the book which was the pretty nearly inevitable outcome of Buber's reflections on what it is to be really human and on the community which yields that result—the book that was to be his main contribution to the renewal of European philosophy. The small volume on which Buber had worked for many years bore the title *Ich und Du*, and it appeared simultaneously with Sigmund Freud's *Das Ich und das Es*. What constitutes "being human" is dialogue, a living together with the other, encountering the other and not having him at one's beck and call. The creative but solitary man of idealism is not the real man. The dialogue-motif was worked out in greater detail and formulated more exactly later on in short books like *Zwiesprache* (1932) and

Die Frage an den Einzelnen (1936), and it was an element in all the books that Buber wrote after 1923.

In the same year Buber became an instructor at the *Frei Jüdische Lehrhaus* in Frankfurt-am-Main, where he was also appointed to teach the philosophy of the Jewish religion and ethics. In Frankfurt he met Franz Rosenzweig with whom in 1925 he started translating the *Tenach* (the Old Testament). This work, begun as a joint venture, Buber continued with alone after Rosenzweig's death in 1929, and in 1937 Lambert Schneider of Berlin brought out in fifteen volumes a translation of the Old Testament that can be regarded as among the most important contributions to the modern study of the Bible, *Monumentum Judaicum*.

In the meantime the Jewish settlements in Palestine were growing larger and more numerous, and in 1925 the Hebrew University was founded in Jerusalem. But the relations between Jew and Arab became worse and worse, and when Buber visited Jerusalem in 1927 he sounded an emphatic note of admonition:

> The watchword is service to the foreign peoples living in the land, for the sake of the community (*Gemeinwesen*) which must be brought to birth here; there must be created a link between their interests and ours—but also the furtherance of their distinctive interests in order to make them realize that their standing and working together with us is not only desirable but also possible. For their well-being must also be our concern. They are part and parcel of the community which must come into being here!

However, Buber's task lay not in Palestine but in Europe. There he breathed his native air in the world of religious socialism and struck up a friendship with the Swiss theologian, Leonhard Ragaz. It was in this period that he parted once for all with the Zionist movement, which had indeed "conformed" and now considered a Jewish State in Palestine to be the unquestioned goal of its activity.

In 1933 Hitler came to power in Germany, but Buber remained there until 1938. Meanwhile Buber's first major book on the Old Testament—*Königtum Gottes* (1932,[2] 1936)—appeared, along with an important collection of speeches and articles, *Die Stunde und die Erkenntnis* (1936), which made it clear that

Buber had no illusions about the intentions of the Third Reich. In 1938 he left Germany, after being nominated to a chair of general sociology at the Hebrew University in Jerusalem—a post he assumed soon after the Austrian Anschluss, on April 25, 1938.

But Buber's life was not now devoted to concentrated academic work alone. In Palestine he continued to do his utmost, to create a good relationship, a condition of "peaceful co-existence", between Jew and Arab. One piece of evidence for this is his *Arab-Jewish Unity: Testimony before the Anglo-American Inquiry Commission for the Ihud (Union) Association by Judah Magnes and Martin Buber* (1947). And the ideal at which the Jewish community in Palestine had to aim was formulated again in *Netiwoth be-Utopia* (1947) = *Pfade in Utopia* (1950). But things did not go at all as Buber had envisaged. In 1948 the State of Israel was proclaimed and the conflict between Jews and Arabs began. Israel had come to be "like all peoples"—and in that regard, it must be observed that at that moment there was no alternative!

During and after the war a number of other books by Martin Buber appeared which we propose to discuss later: in 1942 *Thorath ha-Nebi'im* (=*Der Glaube der Propheten*, 1950); in 1943 *Baajath ha-adam* (= *Das Problem des Menschen*, 1948); in 1945 *Mosche* (a book that has been translated into many languages); in 1947 *Netiwoth be-Utopia* (to which we have already referred); in 1950 *Zwei Glaubensweisen* (a study of the New Testament and of the meaning of faith for Judaism as compared with its meaning for Christianity); in 1952 *Die chassidische Botschaft;* in 1953 *Gottesfinsternis.*

Beginning in 1962, Kösel Verlag in Munich and Lambert Schneider in Heidelberg brought out an edition of Martin Buber's works in three volumes; this edition presents a collection of Buber's principal writings but does not include his translation of *Tenach.*

Martin Buber died on Saturday, June 12, 1965, in Jerusalem in the State of Israel. He was 87 years of age. At the funeral of this man who was the greatest Jewish thinker of the 20th century, the government of Israel was not represented.

The Faith of Israel

The essay in which Buber summed up what he had to say about the origin and essential character of Israel's religion first appeared in a Dutch translation. He had written it at the request of G. van der Leeuw for the work entitled *De godsdiensten der wereld* (*The Religions of the World*), which came out in 1940. In the first edition the essay was still not complete, because on May 10, 1940 The Netherlands had become involved in the war and it was no longer possible for the final chapters which had been sent off from Jerusalem to reach the editor. They were incorporated in the second edition.

The initial part of the argument was in the nature of an attempt to explore the mysterious origins of Israelite religion. As in *Königtum Gottes*, so here Buber takes a passage from the Book of Judges as his point of departure. On this occasion the Song of Deborah (Judges 5) is regarded from a scholarly standpoint as the trustworthy basis for following a lead back into the past. Buber accepts the view generally held by experts in biblical criticism that the text of Judges 5, in the form in which it has come down to us, is rooted in the period of the events which it celebrates.

This view with regard to the dating of the Song is not incontestable, for there are good arguments to support the thesis that the prose account of what took place in Deborah's time is older than the Song itself. We cannot remark too often, however, that Buber's line of argument stands, even if we do not share some of his critical presuppositions.

The trail followed by Buber, starting from the Song of Deborah, leads by way of the amphictyonic assembly at Shechem (as described in Joshua 24) to the events at and around Sinai during the journeying in the wilderness, as recalled in Exodus. This journey back through history, from Deborah's arrival on the scene to the revelation at the burning bush, was not necessary to establish that Israel's religion had been founded by Moses. There is more unanimity about Moses' role as founder of the religion than about the authenticity of the Song of Deborah. Especially worthy of attention are the pages dealing with Exodus 3. Moses receives his call at Horeb, the mountain of the Lord, which is identical with Sinai. The Hebrew word for "bush", *senèh*, can be understood as an allusion to Sinai. What Buber has to say about this revelation is repeated and explained in greater detail in *Mosjèh*, a book published in 1945, in which Buber rightly rejects Freud's hypothesis about Moses' Egyptian origin. His name would not have been connected with the Egyptian word *ms* (=child, from which the associated name of a deity such as Ra or Ptah or Thot must be supposed to have dropped off). The name is a Hebrew participle of a verb meaning "to go forth". *Mosjèh* signifies "one who goes forth", and this name is the title of a savior who rescues his people from a house of bondage and draws them through the waters of the Red Sea to freedom and the promised land.

The divine reality who discloses himself in the fire describes himself before Moses as "the God of your father, the God of Abraham, the God of Isaac, the God of Jacob". This utterance opens a way for Buber to push back to the revelation given to Abraham as the earliest attainable source of Israel's faith. Where this source is concerned—excepting certain finer distinctions and restrictions—there is a large measure of agreement at the present time. The religion of Israel, established as the national religion by Moses, whose ancestry was Levitical, had a prehistory which has been handed down to us in the form of a record of the patriarchs and their religious experiences. Opinion may differ as to whether it was Jacob who actually received the revelation and whether Abraham and Isaac played a more subsidiary role than the record assigns to them. But hardly anyone dissents from the view that the religion founded by Moses is linked with ancient traditions.

According to the tenor of Exodus 3 Moses considered that his mission was not backed by sufficient authority if all that he could tell his compatriots in Egypt was that the God of their fathers had summoned him to his task. The people were bound, he thought, to expect some more precise declaration and to ask *Mah shemo* (customarily translated: "What is his name?") (Ex. 3, 13). The reply to this question was *èhyèh ashèr èhyèh*. On the meaning of this expression there exists a literature of almost unmanageable proportions, which we cannot go into here. As is clear from various early renderings, there has been a protracted effort to arrive at an adequate representation of what these words signify. If we decide to forget all about the literature centered on the expression, we may interpret it in a quite natural way as follows: Moses inquires as to the name of the self-revealing Power, and receives an evasive answer: It makes no difference what I am called; I am who I am. There are parallel evidences to support this interpretation of the text. When Jacob wrestles with a supernatural power by the river Jabbok, he gets no answer to his question about the name either (Gen. 32, 29). The angel who had appeared to Manoah and his wife with a message announcing the birth of Samson, when asked "What is your name?", replies with the enigmatic words: "Why do you ask my name, seeing it is wonderful?" (Jgs. 13, 18).

However, since Buber holds, where the composition of the tradition is concerned, to the final reaction, he is of course bound to assume that the name had been known from the time of the patriarchs. Thus the most that could be required was a more specific explanation. That is why he translates the passage bearing on the question of the name in this way:

Mosche sprach zu Gott: Da komme ich denn zu den Söhnen Jisraels, ich spreche zu ihnen: Der Gott eurer Väter schickt mich zu euch, sie werden zu mir sprechen: Was ists um seinen Namen? — was spreche ich dann zu ihnen? Gott sprach zu Mosche Ich werde dasein, als der ich dasein werde.

Moses said to God: When I come therefore to the sons of Israel, and say to them: The God of your fathers has sent me to you, they will say to me: What does his name signify? What am I then to say to them? God said to Moses: I shall be that I shall be.

The weakness of this translation is obvious. The rendering of *mah shemo* as "What does his name signify?" is very forced. E. Auerbach, in his *Moses*—a book published in 1953—rightly rejects such an interpretation. He points out that in Genesis 32, 27 the divine being puts precisely the same question to Jacob, and the latter in reply gives his name. In Proverbs 34, 4 we find the expression: "What is his name, and what is his son's name?" No one—not even Buber—thinks of translating this as: "What is this [name] all about; what does it really signify?"

We can go along with Buber and Rosenzweig, however, when they say that the obscure words *èhyèh ashèr èhyèh* are not to be taken in any philosophical sense, as though they were some kind of pronouncement about "eternal being" or about God's "necessary existence". The Greek translation of Exodus 3, 14— *tō ōn*— had pointed in the wrong direction. In his highly original work *Der Ewige*, Rosenzweig had rightly argued that the wretched and the oppressed in Egypt had little need of a lecture on "the necessary existence of God". To agree with the assertion that even the briefest utterance on the subject of eternal being would have found no response or point of contact in the Egyptian house of bondage is not to say, however, that one approves the odd translation: "What does his name signify?" What we have here is an inquiry as to a name so far undisclosed.

But we have already made the point that rejecting an interpretation, even when it relates to texts of fundamental importance, need not be an obstacle to pursuing the main lines of the investigation. To do so brings us to Abraham, to the encounter of the patriarch with his God.

What Buber has to say on this topic is central to his understanding of what "believing" is in general. It is not to be isolated from what was embodied in the document entitled *Ich und Du*. The relation between I and Thou is actualized in Abraham's faith. It is beyond us to determine whether Abraham was truly the first to become involved in the inexhaustible dialogue of God with man. In the recorded biblical tradition he was the first, if we accept that history in the generally prevailing sense of the word begins with the stories of Abraham.

Buber seldom mounts a line of argument without reacting, either positively or negatively, to the most important literature provided by critical scholarship on the subject in question. What he has to say about "the God of Abraham" is in large measure inspired by Albrecht Alt's study, *Der Gott der Väter*. Using Greek-language inscriptions of an early date, Alt had shown that the expression "God of N.N." is to be traced back to the religious experience of an individual confronted with a power that is nameless yet discloses itself as personal. This N.N. describes his experience to his family, his clan, and since he is a person vested with authority, the family or clan follows him in venerating a divine being who is henceforward invoked as "the God of N.N.". Buber parts company with Alt insofar as the latter is not prepared to recognize the experiences of Isaac and Jacob as distinct evidence, but he follows in the main the conception that Alt had formed as to the origin of the worship of *theoi patroioi*—named after people who had had an encounter with some divine power.

A second motif in Buber's view of things is afforded by a piece of evidence that we owe to the excavations carried out in the Near East. We now know that the South Mesopotamian city of Ur used to be a center of the cult of the moon god, Sin. This town has been identified, though not on very good grounds, with Ur-Kasdim-Ur of the Chaldees—which, according to a statement preserved in the Hebrew text but in fact very much open to question, was Abraham's place of origin. The Greek version avoids mentioning Ur, and ancient rabbinical exegesis, preserved in the Targum, speaks of "the oven of the Chaldees", not of a city of Ur. Thus the tradition that Abraham, the son of Terah, hailed from Ur rests on weak textual evidences. That is why it is also wrong, simply on the grounds that Ur is mentioned, to suppose that Terah worshiped the moon god. Furthermore, Terah's clan does not give the impression of ever having included city dwellers. It is more to the point that the northern center of the Aramaeans, Haran, possessed an influential moon cult, and here we stand on firmer ground insofar as information regarding the patriarchs' country of origin is concerned. At any rate they came from an area where the moon cult was widespread.

Thus, it is against this background—of the *theoi patroioi* and of the moon cult—that we must read the passage in *The Faith of Israel* where the appeal to argument gives place to a style of special pleading. Buber cites the assyriologist Dhorme, who had called the moon "the god of the Mesopotamian nomads" and "preparer of the way for the caravan, which in order to elude the burning heat of the sun travels across the steppes by night". In keeping with that point of view is the following passage: "My view may be called rationalistic: it seems to me something tremendous in the history of religion that a roving Aramaean should abandon the faith, taken over from his surroundings, in 'the planet of way for the wayfaring Semitic race' (Doughty) and believe in one who was no 'nature god' but a mighty, invisible and yet public guardian God: not the god of the Terahites but the God of Abraham and of his newly errant stock and of all associated with him. A God who is protector and traveling companion, not only on moonlit nights, but even on those days when the nomad of the Mesopotamian steppes elects to journey by day. A God whose light does not wane. A God in whom men put their trust because he speaks to them. He is a God who tells man that he is leader and guide—but taking him where? Not whither a man would wish to come. He leads man to the place whither he sends him. He brings somebody safely to Haran, and there that man settles down; there he would remain. But God wills otherwise. God sends him on his way—out from the paternal home and into a strange country, which is the country of his promise. He turns a man into a wanderer, a nomad of faith."

Albrecht Alt had earlier described in detail the character of the cult of the *theoi patroioi*. He had made a special point, for example, of the fact that a cult of this kind is very adaptable to changes in the social and economic environment. The nomad who becomes semi-nomadic, and the semi-nomad who becomes accustomed to a settled life of husbandry, can venerate the *theos patroios*, whatever the circumstances and whatever the changes that take place. His religion is unaffected by his altered surroundings. The cult is not tied to a particular cultic spot or even to a national boundary. The Lord who is worshiped moves hither and thither with his people. He is a "migrant God", present in Haran and in the Syrian desert, in Egypt as well as in Canaan.

Buber endorses and elaborates upon all this, but anyone familiar with the backgrounds of his ideas about the philosophy of religion will be aware that he contributes a different emphasis. Abraham's encounter with his God is not only a revelation of the "migrant God" who roams with the nomad along the borders of the steppe and the settled, agricultural land. What the encounter exemplifies above all is *the* typical feature of devotion in the Bible: the life of dialogue. Abraham is conscious of being addressed by a Power who reveals himself as a Person and recognizes and treats his human partner in the conversation as a person. Through the medium of intelligible human language Abraham is involved in a persisting conversation—a conversation that can assume every form possible in human dialogue also. It is not simply a matter of God imparting his will and getting an obedient response. Thus in commenting upon Jeremiah's dispute with his God, Buber has this to say: "Man, to whom and through whom the Word is spoken, is above all else a person; before it is spoken through him in human language, it is uttered to him in another language, from which he has to transpose it into the human variety. To be able to speak to men God must become a person—but he must also make a person of man. This human person does not simply receive the Word; he also responds, complaining, accusing God himself, contending with him over the rights and wrongs, submitting, entreating. Of all the prophets of Israel Jeremiah is alone in having dared to record this audacious and zealous and living dialogue of one who is absolutely subject with the One who is absolutely sovereign; to such a degree has the human being become a person that the dialogue here has developed into its purest form. Man can speak and he may speak, and so long as he is truly speaking to God, there is nothing that he may not say to him."

This pronouncement evidently has in view two verses from Jeremiah: (1) "Why is my pain unceasing, and my wound incurable, refusing to be healed? Wilt thou be to me like a deceitful brook, like waters that fail?" (Jer. 15, 18); (2) "Righteous art thou, O Lord, when I complain to thee: yet I would plead my case before thee. Why does the way of the wicked prosper? Why do all who are treacherous thrive?" (Jer. 12, 1). This dialogue, which is not held in check by any slavish submissiveness to a divine will, assumes a literary form in the utterances of the plaintive and protesting Job. The book in its present form is inconceivable apart from the religious perception that the Lord will tolerate the fiercest and most disputatious argument when it is still a conversation with him.

These aspects—the God who is the "traveling companion" and the "life of dialogue"—are the principal elements in Buber's account of Israel's faith. Around them a number of exegetical issues have clustered, which one can accept or reject without invalidating the kernel of his argument. They testify to the stupendous range of his reading and to an unrivaled ability to get under the skin of the Hebrew text. In no instance is his exposition disengaged; it always bears upon him personally, upon his people, upon that people's calling and mission. He opens up what is inscribed in Holy Scripture, but is at the same time a preacher who addresses himself to his people in order to summon them back under the "yoke of the revelation that is both gift and demand".

This preaching activity of his is at its most impressive in what he has to say regarding the servant of the Lord in Deutero-Isaiah, as it is called. In Isaiah 49, 1-7, the servant compares himself to an arrow that has not been shot off, an arrow concealed in God's quiver. He has labored in vain. Yet he is comforted by the message that a task awaits him, a task far greater than all the rest. In a new world that is coming into existence among men, the most distant nations shall hear his message. In the event kings shall arise and worship the Holy One of Israel, he will become a light to the *goyim*.

Here again there is no question of a detached, non-commital exegesis of the text of Isaiah 49. The servant is Israel, with its secret mission for the world, and each phase in the history of the diaspora is to be distinguished by whether it has borne with patience the *Leidenstiefe* (depth of passion) of the prophets' faith or has renounced it.

The Theocracy

In 1932 a book by Martin Buber about the religion of Israel appeared under the title *Königtum Gottes*. It was advertised as the first part of a trilogy on the overall theme of *Das Kommende. Untersuchungen zur Entstehungsgeschichte des messianischen Glaubens (That Which Is To Come. An Examination of the Origins of Messianic Belief)*. The two volumes that were to form the sequel to this never appeared. From the fragments that came out in advance of the definitive edition, however, one can form a clear idea of their intended content. Certain chapters of the second volume are to be found in a 1951 Festschrift dedicated to the German New Testament scholar, Ernst Lohmeyer, and also in a few periodicals. The second half of the long essay, *The Faith of Israel*, deals with what should have formed the substance of the final volume of the trilogy.

From the very beginning, therefore, it had been Buber's intention to write about the messianic expectation; thus we can regard his *Königtum Gottes* as an attempt to explore the sources of that messianic longing which became in the course of history so marked a feature of the Jewish religion.

Buber's characteristic method in building up an argument is to take as his starting point a text that he holds to be contemporaneous in the form in which it has reached us with the events to which it alludes. In the case of the issues under discussion in *Königtum Gottes* this passage is Judges 8, 22-23: "Then the men of Israel said to Gideon, 'Rule thou over us, both you and your son and your grandson also; for you have delivered us out of the hand of Midian.' And Gideon said to them, 'I will not rule over you, and my son will not rule over you; the Lord shall rule over you.' "

In interpreting this passage, which he considers to be of such fundamental importance, Buber starts from the conviction that what we are faced with here is a piece of authentic historical

18

evidence from the early history of Israel. According to this the kingship had been offered to the successful commander in a big battle during the period of the Judges, but he had refused to accept it. In Gideon's eyes an earthly kingship would have been incompatible with a theocracy.

According to the notion that Buber had formed on the basis of various bits of information in the Bible, the theocracy was part and parcel of the circumstances prevailing in the desert period. It was a theocracy in the true and original sense of the word, and for Israel that meant in practice that the whole of her political life was subject to the discipline of God's control. This subjugation to the kingly rule of God was not put into practice by means of a hierocracy, with a hereditary priestly dynasty wielding political power. Israel's unique situation was the result of an absolute commitment to the will of Yahweh.

This commitment, this surrender to the governance of God at the national as well as the individual level, is without parallel in history, and it continued up to the time of Saul and David. Until the period of the kings, Israel was fully dedicated to the idea of a pure theocracy. Gideon's declaration was the proof of this.

Many biblical scholars and critics have regarded Gideon's utterance as a theological datum, not as a piece of historical evidence. The remark about the rule of God must have been put into the judge's mouth by a later generation. In an appendix to the second edition of 1936 Buber defended his point of view at some length, deploying a number of scholarly arguments. According to him the theocracy had been deeply rooted in the period after the exodus from Egypt. Joshua had not appointed a successor, because the leadership in Israel had to be entrusted to men and women who had been moved by *ru'ah*—that is, by the "spirit" of Yahweh.

The instruments of this *ru'ah*—as mysterious in its operation as the wind, of which men know not whence it comes nor whither it goes—are not the priests. They owe their function to their ancestry and maintain a continuity in the exercise of religion; in virtue of a certain knowledge and training handed down from generation to generation they are able to supply the answer to problems put to them, but political leadership they are unable to give, particularly in the critical situations that confront Israel in

Canaan. In times of distress and turmoil the leadership passed to
prophets and Nazirites. It was *ru'ah* that made them into deliverers. We can tell this even now from Amos 2, 10-11, for example:

> Also I brought you up out of the land of Egypt,
> and led you forty years in the wilderness,
> to possess the land of the Amorite.
> And I raised up some of your sons for prophets,
> and some of your young men for Nazirites.
> Is it not indeed so, O people of Israel? says the Lord.

These words of Amos, uttered in the middle of the 8th century
B.C., still link the struggle against the Amorites during the conquest of Canaan with the activities of prophets and Nazirites.
Amos from Tekoa, who expressly dissociates himself from
prophets and the sons of the prophets, sees the part they had
formerly played as a special favor bestowed in the desert period.
They are bracketed together: the prophet who was inspired by
ru'ah and the Nazirite who drank no wine. The latter was still
seen in Amos' day as one set apart to engage in holy warfare and
obliged, therefore, to keep certain vows. He was not permitted to
drink any product of the vine, and he was obliged to let his hair
grow. He was still the typical Nazirite dedicated to war. But
more important and more active still was the role of the prophet.

With the example of Deborah in view it has of course been
contended that the prophet was required to spur on the deliverers
of the nation and to celebrate their deeds. In the song that has
come down to us in Judges 5, Deborah did indeed celebrate the
deliverance, and she did also encourage Barak. However, it is
expressly stated that she was a "prophetess" who "judged" the
people. From this we can conclude that in the tradition about
Deborah some prefatory piece of evidence is missing. She could
not be called "prophetess" unless, like the judges, she had been
possessed by *ru'ah*. It is stated of all the judges that the spirit had
impelled them to action when their people were in great danger.
Even a figure like Samson could not have been a judge apart from
the inscrutable working of the Spirit, entering into possession
now of this person, now of that, and making of them an instrument of the divine will. Samson was not a "deliverer" in the
struggle with the Philistines because he was so strong but rather

because the *ru'ah* was ready to make use of his strength (Judges 13, 15; 14, 19).

Thus it is possible more or less to summarize the notion that Buber entertains of the political and religious situation in the period preceding the inauguration of the kingship. According to him the history of that time had not been rewritten by a later generation from a theocratic viewpoint, but Judges does afford a reliable picture of the period in which the struggle to make theocracy a reality over the whole field of political life took place. What the tradition of the pre-Davidic period presents is simply a "receiving of charisma" in the manner of the prophets. Historically speaking, the traditional must be absolutely trustworthy. God rules through the medium of the judge endowed with "spirit", and the judge has no need of any priest as an intermediary or oracular mouthpiece, over and above himself.

It is a pity that in Gideon's utterance the word *mèlèch* (= king) does not occur. When he speaks of *mashal* (= ruling), it is of course to the function of the *mèlèch* that he refers. The divine *mèlèch* does not in principle tolerate any human *mèlèch* alongside himself. So much is definitely presupposed in what Gideon says, for the hereditary character of a dynasty is mentioned as a distinctive mark of the authority to rule. Hereditary succession, the *droit de naissance*, offers no guarantee at all, however, of the working of the Spirit. Because Yahweh alone is *mèlèch* of Israel and no one else can assume that position, it is necessary to wait for whomever the God of Israel will select as leader, judge and deliverer.

This unique relationship between Yahweh and his people does not mean that other nations also cannot be led into a good country by the same God. He brought Israel out of the Egyptian house of bondage, but according to Amos he also brought the Philistines out of Caphtor and the Aramaeans out of Kir (Amos 9, 7). The Philistines and the Aramaeans, however, did not in consequence of this come to worship the God who had so led them out, and so it could never, in their case, have led to its logical conclusion in a theocracy. The foundation of the theocratic idea is a given historical event: the exodus from the house of bondage in Egypt. Thereafter Israel worships the God whose actions in history prove to be a matter of experience.

Where the relationship between God and nation is concerned, Buber attaches great importance to the institution of the royal covenant, as described in Exodus 24, 7. When in this connection he uses the expression *sakral-rechtlicher Gegenseitigkeitsakt* (a deed of reciprocity—i.e., a reciprocal enactment having a sacral-cum-judicial character), he is uttering words of almost incalculable consequence. What is stated here is crucial for Buber's way of envisaging the relationship of God and man in Israel's religion.

According to what we read in Exodus 24, 6-7, Moses divided into halves the blood of the sacrificed animals. One half he sprinkled on the altar; the other was kept for a time in a basin and afterward sprinkled over the people. In the interval between the rites Moses read out the words of "the book of the covenant". When the people had solemnly undertaken to obey such commandments and prohibitions as were ordered in the book, they were sprinkled with the blood while Moses uttered the formula: "Behold the blood of the covenant which the Lord has made with you in accordance with all these words."

This ritual must be unique not only in the history of religions but even within the Old Testament itself. Nowhere else—so Buber declares—do we find any account of a sacral transaction at all comparable with this ceremony. There are analogous rites where it is a matter of a covenant concluded between human beings—but not in respect of the sort of bond, forged mutually between God and man, that according to Exodus 24 was effected on Sinai. That he is very much aware of the sweep of this interpretation and what it implies appears from the argumentation which, after a lengthy and detailed exchange with the exegetes, recapitulates: Only in the covenant on Sinai is a sacred transaction concluded which on a sacramental basis "constitutes a reciprocal relation between the One above and something below".

In direct line with this unique covenant between God and his people stand the words of Deuteronomy 33, 5: "Thus the Lord became king in Jeshurun, when the heads of the people were gathered, all the tribes of Israel together." Jeshurun is a name for Israel. There is an ironic reference to it in Deuteronomy 32, 15: "But Jeshurun waxed fat, and kicked; you waxed fat, you grew thick, you became sleek; then he forsook God who made him, and scoffed at the Rock of his salvation." Buber opposes the interpretation of Deuteronomy 33, 5 according to which the Song of Moses anticipates the establishment of the kingship. On the contrary, the text is looking back to the ideal period in the desert when Yahweh had assumed the kingship. How we date the Book of Deuteronomy is neither here nor there, so far as this exegesis is concerned. Even if Deuteronomy were drafted wholly in the 7th century B.C., it is still possible to regard Yahweh's kingship as a presupposition. In a positive sense it meant that for as long as this world should last Israel had submitted itself to the will of the *mèlèch*, Yahweh. Negatively, it implied that the nation was to eschew the establishment of a hereditary dynasty, because whether it were of kings or of priests, it could afford no guarantee that the divine *ru'ah* would be received. Thus the period from Joshua to Saul and David has to be viewed in the light of the struggle to preserve and maintain the theocracy.

One may indeed go along with Buber's view of this provided that one starts from certain assumptions about the biblical texts on which the argument is constructed. One finds that practically no use is made, for instance, of the source-hypothesis. The issue has nothing to do—as Buber and Rosenzweig have said—with the sources (Yahwist [J], Elohist, Deuteronomist or Priestly Code) which since the publication of Astruc in 1753 have more and more come to dominate the initiatory study of the Old Testament, as names attached to cycles of traditions which were merged into the Pentateuch and were a factor in the final redaction of Joshua and Judges. Over against these, the only relevant source is the one that they call "R", denoting the latest redactor. For them this R source was also *Rabbenu*—that is, "our master". The picture of Israel's religion in its earliest recoverable period is formed quite deliberately, therefore, on the version of it presented by the latest redactor.

In respect to this, it may be objected that the editor in question, out of prejudice and viewing everything from the angle of prophetic ideals and aspirations, projects the real theocracy into the period of Joshua and the Judges. What to his mind was politically an ideal state of affairs he antedates as a situation prevailing in the desert period and the years subsequent to it. It was a prophetic viewpoint, therefore, that was imposed quite consciously upon the early history of Israel.

Buber completely inverts the theory that the ideal state of affairs has been antedated. The account of the desert period, the conquest of the country and the period of the Judges was not molded by the prophets into the form in which it has been transmitted to us. On the contrary, the phenomenon of prophetism is inexplicable if Israel's history did not happen—at least where its main features are concerned—basically as the tradition conjures it up for us.

Enshrined in the tradition is the memory of the crisis that descended upon the theocracy under the pressure of circumstances. The widely scattered tribes were scarcely able to stand up for themselves against the invading nomads—and even less so against the ever deeper incursions of the Philistines into the country. Apparently, a few judges were able now and then to unite one or two tribes in a defensive alliance and to ward off an enemy. In certain places they effected a limited and temporary solution. Where they did appear on the scene, however, the signs were evident enough that the *ru'ah* of Yahweh was blowing. From this charisma they took their authority and also their right to have themselves described as judges over the whole of Israel. It is true that their power extended over no more than a handful of tribes, but from a theocratic viewpoint Israel can only be said to be present where Yahweh is king—and so the whole of Israel is there represented. Deborah—who, as we know, headed only a couple of northern tribes—is nevertheless for that reason rightly described as a "mother in Israel" (Jgs. 5, 7).

But under the pressure of the Philistine invasions the people's demand that a king be chosen becomes more and more insistent. This king is then to take command in the war thrust upon Israel, under the stress of which she is threatening to collapse. The pressure put on Samuel by the people can no longer be withstood by this last representative of the theocratic age. Even though it is expressly said of Saul that after his anointing by Samuel he was seized by *ru'ah* (1 Sam. 10, 10) and made to participate in the ecstatic frenzy of a group of prophets who were passing by, the inauguration of the kingship is seen as an encroachment upon the pure form of theocracy.

From this moment on, the role of the prophet in Israel was that of one who was there with the king in order to pass judgment on his actions. The prophet had this authority because he was the instrument of the same *ru'ah* which in earlier times had motivated the judges. He was authoritative precisely because he perpetuated the traditions of the theocracy in this respect. David recognized this in Nathan, for instance, when in a catastrophic situation the prophet stood over against the king. Ahab, too, bowed to the authority of Elijah, and it may well be legitimate in that connection to ask whether in the northern kingdom the authority of the prophet, acting in the name of Yahweh, was not stronger even than in Jerusalem, where since the time of Solomon syncretism had made deep inroads. It was also in the north, in the kingdom of the ten tribes, that in the middle of the 8th century B.C. a prophet like Hosea could recall the time of the journeying through the wilderness as a period when the relationship between the nation and its God was still wholesome and unbroken. The conduct of the prophets as men who urged a return to the theocracy led of necessity to tragic conflicts with the human *mèlèch*.

Buber's way of interpreting the tradition means that we can no longer speak of a "prophetic version" of Israel's earliest history, but must speak instead of a history from which the phenomenon of prophetism was bound to arise. This takes for granted, of course, that in its main features the tradition is historically trustworthy. That tradition may have been handed down over a considerable time by word of mouth, but there is no reason why oral tradition should be *more* exposed to the process of subtle change and transformation than the written one.

Having clearly identified the main trends in Buber's *Königtum Gottes*, we are in a better position to understand why the work in which he seeks to sum up the faith of Israel should bear such titles as *Der Glaube der Profeten*, *Prophetic Faith* and *Thorath ha-Nebi'im*. His overall view takes little account of the contribution made to Israel's religion by the cult or of its role as an element imparting cohesion and unity. As Buber saw it, the cult was too static for the purpose and failed in too many aspects to bring out the distinctive character of Israel. The temple worship had an observable beginning and ending. The existence of a temple, the ministry of the priests and the ritual sacrifices did not ensure the safety and continuance of Jerusalem and Judah.

This also makes it clear why *Königtum Gottes* appeared as the first part of a trilogy intended to describe and account for the origins of messianic belief. That is made plain in the closing sentence: *"Der Gedanke der monarchischen Einung wird geboren und erhebt sich den Vertretern des Gotteskönigtums entgegen. Und die Krisis zwischen beiden wird zu einer des theokratischen Antriebs selber, zu der Krisis, aus der der menschliche König von Israel, der Nachfolger Jhwh's, als dessen Gesalbter, 'meschiach Jhwh', 'Christos Kurios', hervortaucht"* (The idea of the unitive rule of a single king is born and springs up as over against the champions of God's kingship. And this crisis between the two becomes one of the theocratic impulse itself—the crisis from which the human king of Israel, Yahweh's successor, emerges as his Anointed, the 'Messiah of Yahweh', 'Christos Kurios' ").

The prophets, therefore, took over the heritage of the theocracy. It was their confrontation with the frailties of the human *mèlèch* that inevitably elicited in them their own vision of the ideal Messiah who was to bring peace to Israel and, through Israel, to the world.

The Translation

Over a period of almost forty years Martin Buber devoted his energies to a new translation of the Bible from Hebrew into German. In an article entitled *Aus den Anfängen unserer Schriftübertragung* (On the Inception of Our Translation of the Scriptures) he tells how it came about that he and Franz Rosenzweig began this gigantic enterprise. Since Rosenzweig died young, one would guess that the burden of the task fell on Buber alone. We must not forget, however, that by the time of Rosenzweig's death the translation, which scrupulously followed the order of the Hebrew Bible, had already been completed as far as Isaiah 53. Furthermore, it is evident from a large number of articles to what a great extent Rosenzweig had set his stamp on the style and choice of vocabulary. When Buber gives Rosenzweig the limelight, this is no exhibition of false modesty on his part.

When the task of translation was begun in the spring of 1925, Rosenzweig had already been incurably ill for some years. From the end of December 1922 he was no longer able to write, and after May 1923 even speech had become impossible. All that he could still do was to point to letters. His wife understood what he meant and set down his ideas in writing. Anyone who reads the letters, poems and articles that Rosenzweig produced in such great numbers must stand amazed at this man. Although his body became gradually more and more disorganized by amyotrophic lateral sclerosis, he felt intensely, and spoke commandingly, about the questions of the day. It was with an equal intensity that he took his share in translating the Bible, while facing up quite consciously to the fact that the end of his life must be very near. That is why he also insisted that on the title page of the first issues of the translation there should be printed the words *Die Schrift zu verdeutschen unternommen* (i.e., he had set out to put the Scriptures into German).

Franz Rosenzweig died on December 10, 1929. A few hours previously he had dictated to Martin Buber a letter—again using sign language—but the dictation was interrupted by the doctor's arrival and was never completed. The contents of this moving document include the words: *"Und jetzt kommt sie, die Pointe aller Pointen, die der Herr mir wirklich im Schlaf verliehen hat: die Pointe aller Pointen für die es. . . ."* ("And now comes the most important point of all, which the Lord actually imparted to me in my sleep: the point of all points for which it. . . ."). That sentence was broken off as Rosenzweig expired.

In a spirit of great fidelity to his colleague, Buber continued with the work of translating. The principles governing the technique of translation had been settled, and no further changes in method were made. It was Rosenzweig who had thought out the German equivalents of many terms, especially those relating to the temple and to the sacrificial cult.

A work that initially had claimed to be no more than a revision of Luther's translation turned out, of intrinsic necessity, to be something different. The respect paid—and it was indeed repeatedly and openly expressed—to Luther's translation did not mean that the Hebrew Bible was not put into German here in a wholly distinctive fashion and in a version that was independent and genuinely new. Was this typically modern German, employing the speech of the 20th century? That it certainly was not. No attempt was made to translate the Bible into simple, current German, for Holy Writ has never been simple or "current" in form or content. It had been agreed between the two men that in translating they would follow as faithfully as they could the words of the original text, both with respect to their sequence and to the general tone of their etymological background. This meant in practice that they forced the German language into the mold of Hebrew idiom, right up to the limits which the syntax and vocabulary of a language tied to European culture will permit.

At a time when the tides of overwrought nationalism were rising in Germany, this was a very risky thing to do. The target of the criticism that would be aimed at the translation was foreseeable from the start; foreseeable, too, was the quarter from which the wind of criticism would blow.

That—given the method—there could be no question of a supple and readable text was settled in advance. The translation did not set out to be an interpretation. What it did offer, however, was the concentrated wisdom of centuries of biblical exegesis, set down in commentaries, from the earliest Jewish and Christian interpretations of the text right up to the most modern insights and opinions. Only the expert, therefore, can have some idea of what searching enquiry and what amount of wrestling with both languages lie behind this or that apparently obvious rendering. Yet even the most ingenuous reader must feel something of this when he reads, for instance, the opening sentences:

Im Anfang schuf Gott den Himmel und die Erde.
Und die Erde war Irrsal und Wirsal.
Finsternis über Urwirbels Antlitz.
Braus Gottes spreitend über dem Antlitz der Wasser.

In the beginning God created the heavens and the earth.
And the earth was chaos and confusion.
Darkness [lay] over the face of the primeval whirlpool,
Tumult of God spreading over the face of the water.

The text was intended to be read aloud. The translators did not merely want to translate word for word, but to convey a rhythm that would do justice to the use of the pericopes in the original. They were not meant to be read silently, as we have normally been reading since Augustine's day. The original way of reading was to recite aloud, and where the text was read in a religious community, it was lightly intoned, almost sung. That is another reason why the text is not an easy one for people nowadays who are accustomed to seeing thousands of written words flit past day after day. Of those words only a quintessential—or supposedly quintessential—few remain as ideas in the mind. When the written word was something rare and therefore very precious, it was pondered over and over again. The activity of reading was more what we today would call "close reading". It was not at all a matter of flitting cursorily through page after page *ad infinitum* and trying somehow to digest them. But it was with such "close reading" in view that the text of Holy Scripture was put into book form and so handed down, and the task of the good exegete

is to read again, as men used to read when writing was a youthful
and marvelous art, a progression of spellbinding texts by means of
which the soul of man could journey forth into the uttermost
reaches of time and space. The runes of the divine revelation are
the vehicles of a mystery still more profound—something to be
deciphered rather than read and heard.

The translation by Buber and Rosenzweig compels the reader
to imbibe, to *taste* the words—but deliberately, slowly, without
gulping them down, almost as people before printed books were
invented would take their time over letting a passage penetrate
their minds and so would become, as it were, one with the word
itself.

Can we say that the German employed here is nevertheless a
pure kind of German? Rosenzweig especially had given such
weight to the etymology of the words that the German equivalents inevitably seem forced and artificial. A few examples will
serve to illustrate this.

Koehler and Baumgartner's standard lexicon rightly says of the
Hebrew word *corban* that it is a very general and colorless term
for an offering. It is a typical word in the vocabulary of the
temple, and outside the books of Leviticus and Numbers it hardly
appears. Etymologically, it is connected with the verb *carab*
which means "to approach". A *corban*, therefore, in the original
sense of the word, is that which enables an approach to be made
to the altar, the priests, the godhead. In Buber and Rosenzweig's
translation the word is rendered as *Darnahung* (a "drawing
near"), and this is an expression that will not immediately mean
so much to the reader as the normal translation, "offering"—
although the association with the Latin *offerre* (to present) usually escapes us. But must a word make its significance felt
straightaway? The reader is often poorly nourished with words
that are all too easy to digest.

The translation using the peculiar-sounding word *Darnahung*
was justified on the strength of Numbers 16: the story of the
three rebels, Korah, Dathan and Abiram. The word *corban* does
not occur in this chapter, but what does occur a number of times
is the verb *carab*, in its expressly cultic sense of "to approach the
altar". Thus we read: "And he said to Korah and all his company,
'In the morning the Lord will show who is his, and who is holy,

and will cause him to come near to him; him whom he will
choose he will cause to come near to him' " (Num. 16, 5; cf. also
Num. 16, 9). It is indeed evident enough: "to come near" and
"to cause to come near" have a cultic significance. They sound a
note that accords with what the notion of "being far off and
coming near" signified for the idea of "offering" in Israel.

The etymological method is similarly employed to give a typical rendering of a number of other words: *'ōlāh* becomes not
"burnt offering" but *Darhöhung*, because the stem does not mean
"to burn" but "to ascend". *Minchāh* becomes not "meal offering"
but *das Hingeleitete* (that which is led thither) and *misbēach*
becomes not "altar" but *Schlachtstatt* (place of slaughter). Our
rendering of *rēach nichôach* is "sweet smell"; Rosenzweig translates it as *Ruch des Geruhens*. It was an advantage in this connection that Grimm's big dictionary of the German language remained so accommodating and offered a handsome treasury of
words and constructions which sound strange to German ears but
are given some legitimacy by the lexicon. Such a thing would
probably give more difficulty in Dutch. But was it, as a translation, an acceptable rendering into an intelligible and—for purists
—justifiable kind of German? It is not altogether a question for
the outsider to answer, but he should be able to sense what the
reactions of a German reader are to a passage such as this one:
part of the regulations prescribed for the Great Day of Atone-
ment in Leviticus 16, 15-17:

Dann metze er den Bock der Entsündung der des Volkes ist,
er bringe sein Blut innseits des Verhangs,
und er tue mit seinem Blut wie er dem Blut des Farren tat,
er spritze es an das Verdeck und vor das Antlitz des Verdecks.
So bedecke er
über dem Heiligtum
vor den Makeln der Söhne Jissraels
und vor ihren Abtrünnigkeiten,
all ihren Versündigungen,
und ebenso tue er
dem Zelt der Gegenwart
des der einwohnt bei ihnen
inmitten ihrer Makel.
Kein Mensch im Zelt der Gegenwart,
wann er eingeht, zu bedecken im Heiligtum,
bis er heraustritt.

Then let him slaughter the buck of expiation for sin, which is
for the people,
let him bring its blood within the veil,
and do with its blood what he did with the blood of the bullock,
let him sprinkle it on the covering and before the face of the
covering.
So let him cover
over the holy place
because of the blemishes of the sons of Israel
and because of their rebellious doings,
all their sins,
and likewise let him do
to the tent of the presence
which dwells with them
amid their shortcoming.
No man in the tent of presence,
when he goes in, to cover within the holy place,
until he steps out.

The same passage in the New Translation commissioned by the
Netherlands Bible Society runs as follows:

Then shall he slaughter the buck of the sin-offering, intended for
the people, and bring its blood within, behind the veil, and do
with that blood as he did with the blood of the bull: he shall
sprinkle it upon the mercy-seat and before the mercy-seat. Thus
shall he make expiation throughout the holy place for the uncleanness of the Israelites and for their transgression in all their
sins; likewise shall he do with the tent of meeting, that abides
with them amid their uncleanness. No person is to be within the
tent of meeting when he enters into it to make expiation in the
holy place, until he comes out.

A count shows that the 53 words of the Hebrew text are
rendered by Buber and Rosenzweig with 95 and in the Dutch
translation with 112, whereas, generally speaking, when Dutch is
translated into German, the text is lengthened by something in
the region of 20%. That Hebrew needs noticeably fewer words is
due to the constructions that enable a preposition, an article and
pronouns to be combined with a substantive in a single expression. If we discount this factor, we cannot but be impressed by
the pregnant force of expression of the German translation. Yet

was the language used in this *Verdeutschung* of the Scriptures in fact any real variety of German?

I note Gerhard Kittel's reaction in an appendix to the second edition of his now notorious work *Die Judenfrage* (*The Jewish Question*). In it he says that he personally has no *Verhältnis*, no fondness whatsoever for Buber's translation, which "despite the German words is as foreign [to him] as the original Hebrew text". And he goes on to say: "I have read a critique of their Bible translation, in which it is compared as a linguistic achievement to Luther's work. That seems to me like comparing fish with fowl." Thus commented Gerhard Kittel, whose words are not to be dissociated from his commitment to national socialism, which made it impossible for him to see in Judaism and its expressions anything other than a world absolutely alien to the German temperament. And others had expressed themselves in the same vein as Kittel—for instance, Wilhelm Stapel in his work *Antisemitismus und Antigermanismus*, published in 1928, where he sets out to pillory the language of the translation as a *Halbjargon*, a kind of semi-jargon. It is evident in retrospect that a lot of the criticism voiced in Germany came from a fairly murky source.

It was not unnatural, however, that others also, who were not tainted with the ideology of national socialism, should feel bound to take exception to both the language and the method of the *Verdeutschung:* to the language particularly because Rosenzweig's principles necessarily involved allowing so much weight to the etymology of the words that the German equivalents were bound to give a forced impression.

If we now set aside the arguments derived from the German *Sprachempfinden* (sensitivity about language), regarding them for what they are, one point of criticism still remains to be considered. During the last few decades the meaning of quite a number of important words taken from the *Biblia Hebraïca* has been subjected to detailed examination. We now have monographs on *ru'ah, nephesh, tsedākāh, torāh, lēb, shoeb* and *māshah*, from which we may conclude that there is no single equivalent in the Dutch language for any of them. Their precise meaning differs according to the context in which they occur. What is more, we have to ask what meaning accrues to the etymology of a word in a living language. Whatever the value of etymological investigation and whatever the background of cultural history against which the meaning of words may change, the old adage *verba valent usu* remains true. In deference to this rule the Bible translator must always ask himself: What did this author in his time, in his milieu and in his mode of thinking understand by this or that word, and how can we reflect its import in our language as adequately as possible? That is why the committee in charge of the Netherlands Bible Society translation deliberately rejected the etymological method of Buber and Rosenzweig. Their translation was always on the table during the consultations held by the translators and was indeed continually consulted, but a uniform rendering of the Hebrew words was quite rightly eschewed.

Even on the assumption that what the Bible proclaims is a unity, it is not in practice possible to constantly render the Hebrew words into Dutch by the same equivalents. In order to obviate misunderstanding on the reader's part one must seek— although always with a degree of caution—to give an interpretation. As an example I have chosen Judges 5, 11, where the New Translation reads:

> At the sound of those who beat time at the watering-places there may one sing of the righteous deeds of the Lord, the righteous deeds of his leaders in Israel.

Buber and Rosenzweig translate at this point:

> *Horch,*
> *Taktschlagende zwischen den Tränken!*
> *dort wechselsagen sie seine Bewährungen,*
> *Bewährungen an seiner Bauernschaft in Jisrael.*

> Harken,
> the one who beats time amid the watering places!
> there they exchange tales of his proving acts,
> proofs [offered] to his country folk in Israel.

I pass over such problems in this passage as the rendering of *perazon*—a word occurring only here and in v. 7. The Bible Society's translation is a bold one, and my personal view is that Buber and Rosenzweig's *Bauernschaft* is somewhat easier to justify on philological grounds. Opinion may differ about this, as indeed it did among the members of the translation committee. Again, it is a pity that the Bible Society's statute does not permit it to issue a Bible with marginal notes in which the alternative readings—without which every reader of a translation is going to be misled—can be given. What a text of this sort does serve to demonstrate, however—and this is the important point—is that *tsedākāh* is not to be rendered consistently as "justice", and anyone who does so is simply deceiving the reader. The word calls in this case for some further elucidation, and in my view the expression "righteous deeds" serves the purpose well.

Now it may be said that Buber and Rosenzweig found a happy solution to the problem when they translated *tsedākāh* not as *Gerechtigkeit* (justice) but as *Bewährung* (proof, trial). I ask myself, however, whether even someone whose mother tongue is German is going to be very happy with these *mots justes!*, these lucky finds, in their translation. Admittedly, they could always appeal to Grimm's dictionary and thus maintain against all criticism that they had not coined any new words but had simply drawn on the stock of German words already available; however, not every word in a comprehensive vocabulary is common property. Anyone who wants to produce a popular Bible must take some account of what the average reader can understand. I feel sure that the term *slee* (sloe) instead of *stomp* (stub) in Jeremiah 31, 29-30 must be unintelligible to the majority of people in the west of our country who read the New Translation—unintelligible at any rate without a look at Van Dale's lexicon—even though the word used is in point of fact the only correct one. With regard to Buber and Rosenzweig's translation, it is fair enough to say that it is not to be understood by people who do not know any Hebrew. I can personally vouch for the fact that I was unable to understand some of the passages in this translation properly until I had consulted the original Hebrew text. The translation is designed for an elite and for them is useful as a commentary—a commentary, let it be said, which is extremely valuable and very stimulating, one for which no praise could be too high.

In 1938 a malicious little joke about Buber was making the rounds in Jerusalem—a joke that nevertheless contains a germ of truth. As professor of sociology at the Hebrew University, it was his duty, after a certain length of time, to lecture in Hebrew. When after several months he still persisted in using German, someone asked: "Can't he make himself understood in Hebrew?" Someone else is said to have replied: "Make himself intelligible in Hebrew? Certainly he can! The trouble is he can't make himself *un*intelligible in Hebrew." Buber's language is one that reveals and conceals at the same time. That is something which may well call for a very positive appraisal, for where profound and mysterious matters are in question, we would do better not to allow our speaking to rise above a whisper. The splish-splash of limpid waters is seldom suggestive of tremendous depths, and when we speak in truth about God, we can do little more than "skirt around the subject". It is not difficult to see that the revelations of the Unsearchable are inevitably wrapped in a garment of unsearchability.

But criticism and questioning detract not in the slightest degree from what Rosenzweig called *Das Formgeheimnis der biblischen Erzählungen* (the secret of form in the biblical stories). He has drawn our attention to a peculiar feature of the biblical narrative, which sometimes *"aufgespannt ist auf ein Gerüst einer ganzen Reihe gleicher oder formal zusammenhängender Worte oder auch formelhafter Sätze, die aber unter sich jedes mit dem nächstvorhergehenden wie die Wendungen eines schlagfertigen Dialogs zusammenhängen"* ("is unfolded within the frame of a whole series of like, or formally interrelated, words or even formularized sentences, each of which reciprocally coheres, however, with the one immediately before it, as in the give-and-take of a fast-moving dialogue").

A familiar example of this is the story of Jacob. To the complaining Esau the grey-haired Isaac says of him: "Your brother came with guile, and he has taken away your blessing." Two chapters further on Jacob realizes just how much he is being exploited by his father-in-law, Laban. The "guile" theme then recurs in his words addressed to Laban: "What is this you have done to me? Did I not serve with you for Rachel? Why then have you deceived me?" It was the deceived man who had provided the motif in the first instance—the motif which found an echo in the name "Jacob"—and his deceiver takes it up once more when he in turn becomes the man deceived. It is obvious, of course, that a translator must reckon seriously with such thematic words, which in more cases than the reader often realizes link together extensive parts of the Bible into massive unities.

One of the most significant contributions made by Buber and Rosenzweig's translation is the way in which it deals with the unutterable divine name, the tetragrammaton JHWH. The presumed derivation of the mysterious and unique name of God is not the point of chief importance here. The theory that the source is to be looked for in a *Gottschrei* (divine salutation), Yah or Yahu—which by the addition of an emphatic "*hé*" was turned into a theologoumenon—is one among several. What is really crucial, however, is the fact that the translators broke away from the use of the equivalent, "the eternal", introduced by Mendelssohn in the 18th century and commonly employed since that time in Jewish liturgical literature.

The objections to "the eternal" as a substitute for JHWH are discussed at some length by Rosenzweig, but they are fully supported by the ideas already developed by Buber. The name of Israel's God, whatever its original signification may have been, can never be interpreted by a philosophical concept. God is not "that which is", "the All" or "the ground of things". That is why Mendelssohn's translation—which in point of fact, as the argumentation shows, hangs by no more than a single hair—is misleading. It was an abstract philosophical term which Mendelssohn understood to mean "the eternally necessary" and all too facilely equated with "the providential". As an attribute of God this last is more in keeping with the dynamic character of him who is with his people in Egypt and goes before them through the waters of the Red Sea and, journeying with them into the promised land, is abidingly present in wrath and mercy, arguing and conciliating, concealing and disclosing himself. Against such a background it makes profound sense that the tetragrammaton should be rendered by the capital letters ER in the genitive *Sein* (his) and in the dative *Ihm* (to him).

It had been Buber and Rosenzweig's intention to translate the transmitted Hebrew text without resort to emendations. That is a principle which they share with the (Dutch) States Bible translators as well as with those commissioned by the Netherlands Bible Society. The motives behind a principle of this sort can vary considerably. In Buber and Rosenzweig's case they do not result from a pious veneration of the literal text—the kind of thing that we are familiar with from the Islamic world. The logical outcome of such a reverential attitude must surely be to prohibit translation on religious grounds, and such is in fact the consequence drawn by the followers of Mohammed. In religious use the Koran is recited only in Arabic and without any deviation from the standard text. Christians—for whom the Word became flesh indeed, but not book—have never raised any objection to translation into the language of this or that country, despite the dynamic character with which the Word is thereby endued. Buber and Rosenzweig likewise had no objection to translating as such, and that is in itself a *de facto* disclosure of their free approach to the letter of the book.

Rosenzweig states the issue clearly enough in a letter published in *Der Morgen* for October 1928, where he says: "*Unsre Differenz von der Orthodoxie liegt darin, dass wir aus unserm Glauben an die Heiligkeit, also die Sonderstellung der Tora und an ihren literarischen Entstehungs prozess und über den philologischen Wert des auf uns gekommenen Textes ziehen können. Wenn Wellhausen mit all seinen Theorien recht hätte und wenn die Samaritaner wirklich den besseren Text hätten, würde das unsern Glauben nicht im mindesten berühren*" ("Our difference with Orthodoxy consists in this: that from our belief in the sacredness —and thus the unique status—of the Torah and in its character as revelation, we can draw no conclusions as to the literary process by which it arose and as to the philological value of the text that has come down to us. If Wellhausen were right with all his theories and if the Samaritans really did have the superior text, that would not affect our belief in the slightest").

In principle, therefore, one is at liberty to emend the text on philological grounds. If in fact one does not, that is because the scientific aptitude for so doing is counterbalanced by "*eine ebenso prinzipielle philologische Aengstlichkeit und ein immer waches Misstrauen gegen das notwendig Hypothetische aller Wissenschaft*" ("an equally basic philological scrupulosity and an unremitting suspicion of the necessarily hypothetical character of all scientific knowledge"). In his "Directive for a Bible Course" Buber says that we must be careful to remember that those responsible for the existing form of the Hebrew text have been no less familiar with Hebrew than we are. Therefore, the endeavor to read the Old Testament in Hebrew as it stands is not to be explained in terms of a religious preoccupation.

The person who emends a text is usually making it easy for himself. The help enlisted in the case of *versiones antiquae* runs counter to the rule—not a rule without its exceptions, to be sure—of *lectio ardua praestat*. Anyone who familiarizes himself with the direction taken in general by philology today will soon notice the universal mistrust of emendations. The discoveries made in ancient manuscripts have served to invalidate so many emendations that people have come to adopt an attitude of reserve toward the emending of texts and to concentrate on diplomatic editions. One has to firmly oppose those who are filled with premature rejoicing at the vindication of the religio-conservative standpoint. Between that standpoint and scientific procedure there may well be a point of contact, but this does not in itself vindicate conservatism as a method. That is why Rosenzweig stresses so greatly the distance between himself and what he calls "orthodoxy"—a term that is to be taken here as pointing to Jewish traditionalism. A divergence in matters of principle, however, does not necessarily mean in the majority of cases that no work at the practical level can be done in common. From the viewpoint of Jewish traditionalism it is impossible to object in principle to what Buber and Rosenzweig were seeking with their *Verdeutschung* of the scriptures.

The translators take yet another important step which should find them in good favor with the traditionalists. They take as their starting point what they call "die Einheit der Bibel" ("the unity of the Bible"), envisaging the Bible in this connection as comprising the law, the prophets and the writings. Thus their "unity of the Bible" is something different from the unity of the christological interpretation which reads the books of the Old and New Testaments back to front and offers a Pauline exegesis of the paradise story. Buber and Rosenzweig oppose the atomizing efforts of 19th-century criticism. They are happy enough to recognize that the Torah does not derive from Moses and will concede that the latest redaction of the Bible is an amalgam of many traditions; however, they also maintain—and, in my view, with justification—that the latest redaction of the scriptures is not an arbitrary hodgepodge of traditions. Rosenzweig again puts this very clearly when he says by way of exemplification: "*Hätte die Kritik auch recht und wären Genesis I und II wirklich von verschiedenen Verfassern, so wäre auch dann was uns von der Schöpfung zu wissen nottut, nicht aus einem der beiden Kapiteln allein zu lernen, sondern erst aus ihrem Zusammenstehn und Zusammenklingen*" ("Even if such criticism were to be right, and Genesis 1 and 2 were actually the work of several different people, even then we would learn what we needed to know about the creation not just from one of the two chapters, but only by putting them together and noting their consonance"). Here we come face to face with a crucial act of faith, by which we wish to acknowledge the theology of this latest redactor, identifiable in the unity of the Bible, as our creed and to submit ourselves to it. This commitment of faith has important consequences for the translation. If there is no such thing as a Yahwist or an Elohist theology, if there is no teaching of the Book of Esther to be differentiated from that of Ecclesiastes, we need not trouble ourselves too greatly about the idiom of either of those authors, real or fictitious. In that case we shall not have to ask ourselves, in deciding on the value and significance of what they have to say, whether they lived in the 11th century or in the 4th century. Our business will be to adhere to what we think we have understood to be the intention of the final redactor who serves as our instructor and mentor.

Indeed, we can go further still. The man who posits the unity of the Bible itself may do the same for its interpretation. In the tradition of the Christian Church certain passages have acquired an aura and a significance which interpretation has conferred upon them. A classic example is Joel 2, 23 where "the teacher in righteousness" is in my view entirely out of place with "the torrents of rain". Essentially, the translation of *moré litsdakah* here as "sufficient rain" is the correct one. The rendering "teacher in righteousness" that has now been adopted—one that allows room for ancient christological interpretations—fitted into the unity of the tradition. For Judaism there is a unity of tradition laid down in Talmud and Midrash. One can translate in such a way as still to leave room for their exegesis—at any rate, so as not to controvert it—and to ensure that the translation will not be a "foreign body", something so isolated in its singularity as to be void of all effect. It is fair to say that, despite the revolutionary appearance Buber and Rosenzweig's translation presents, it does fall within the current of Jewish tradition. In the same sense the (Dutch) New Translation on the Protestant side and the Petrus Canisius version on the Roman Catholic side are properly described as traditional. The Leyden translation is not traditional and in that respect has courted what some people—again, from their standpoint, quite justifiably—are going to call a "splendid isolation".

Buber and Rosenzweig have both pointed out repeatedly that their translation is not to be regarded as a non-committal, learned experiment. They have taken the scholarship, the scientific approach, seriously enough. It is no part of their thinking to draw a line between faith and scientific learning, but they are conscious of conducting a systematic study of Holy Writ, actuated by faith and thus accountable to it. They see themselves as people submitted in some inscrutable and nonetheless existential fashion to the Bible. They are governed not by the letter of it but by its message. In the end it is the Bible that directs the translation; this is why Rosenzweig can say: "*Hätte die Bibel nicht diese geheimnisvolle Kraft, unsre Irrtümer in ihre Wahrheit zu verwandeln, so wäre, sie zu übersetzen, ein noch grösseres Wagnis als es das schon ist*" ("If the Bible did not have this mysterious power to transmute our errors into its truth, translating them would be a hazard even greater than it is already").

With these words Rosenzweig captures the note of desperation sounded by every good translator who is unable to draw the distinction between what is "successful" in his work and what is "less successful", but only between what is "wrong" and what is "less wrong". The tract *Soferiem* (1, 7) says that the day on which the Torah was translated into Greek was as black for Israel as the day when the golden calf was made; elsewhere it alleges that at that time darkness reigned over the world for three days. Here, then, in anecdotal form, the terrifying aspect of such a hazardous undertaking as the translating of the Bible is demonstrated. The logical conclusion might be to prohibit it or to leave it alone. That such a conclusion need not be drawn, provided one is conscious of being pupil and servant to the scriptures, is what Rosenzweig, in his well-nigh inimitable way, is saying in the passage to which we have referred. Thus the enterprise, however hazardous, becomes nothing less than an inescapable command.

Chassidism

By Chassidism we are to understand a Jewish mystical movement that arose from the activity of the person known as the Baal Shem Tov in the first half of the 18th century. From the Carpathian area Chassidism spread throughout Poland, Rumania, Hungary and Russia. The movement is so called because its devotees regarded themselves as *Chassidim*. We might translate this self-conferred styling as "pious ones", provided that the term "pious" here is understood not in a context of Jewish orthodoxy but in a mystical-cum-religious sense.

When it is asserted that Buber made Chassidism known in Western Europe, it is necessary to bear in mind a dual proviso. In the first place we must not lose sight of the fact that what so impressed Buber was Chassidism in its first and richest period. Even as early as the start of the 19th century the movement was beginning to assume a certain rigidity, and the representatives of this later period of decline are important only to the extent that in them we may still catch an echo of the pristine enthusiasm. In the second place the critics are correct when they say that Buber's interpretation of the earliest Chassidism cannot always survive a confrontation with the written sources.

It has to be admitted at once that the written tradition gives us nothing reliable to go on when it comes to the life and teachings of the first Chassidic leaders. They put nothing in writing themselves. What they said and did was simply recounted and passed on within the circle of their disciples. The earliest written deposit is to be found in short pamphlets and brochures which are generally considered to have been pretty poor compositions. They are now lost, having been adapted, reissued and radically altered, so that it is hard to tell the more recent layers from the more primitive ones and thus to get back to the original source. The method that Buber employed in this connection was largely intuitive. It is more or less inevitable that his selection, which has passed through the sieve of a powerful personality, should conjure up a one-sided picture.

The great merit of this was that 18th-century Chassidism, for all its strangeness, was communicated in such a way that 20th-century men in Western Europe opened their eyes in astonishment and felt that they were being addressed in person.

This in no way contravened the intentions of the earliest Chassidic instructors, in that they had not in principle proposed any static system; nor did they trouble their heads over the varieties of interpretation given to their sayings by their followers. They lived by the considered opinion that the Talmud had seventy faces and that it is possible to recognize the truth in each of them. Chassidism has a great many aspects, and Buber shows us just a few of them. What we are given to see derives from the interaction which nearly sixty years ago occurred between his spiritual and mental situation and an utterance of the Baal Shem Tov.

This mystic in his testament urges man to stir himself and seek to develop in himself the attribute of zeal. "In zeal he is to rouse himself from sleep; then he will feel himself to be another, a sanctified person, worthy to testify. He is then to be likened with the Holy One—blessed may he be!—when he created the world." Words can get under the skin of a man in an inscrutable and unforeseeable fashion. For Martin Buber this encounter with the words of Baal Shem Tov was like the beginning of a new way. The way of man in accordance with the teaching of the Chassidim was bound to lead to the large-scale religious renewal of Jewry. Liberated from the shackles of traditionalism and legalism, tradition and law would acquire a vital significance, just as the whole of life in its day-to-day character would become transfused with the warmth of a religious joy. That the message of the Chassidic books would make such a deep impression on non-Jewish circles with a strongly religious yearning was hardly to be expected at the beginning of this century.

Moreover, it cannot be said that the legends and parables of the Chassidic writings result in literature that is easily read. Rather than read them casually, it would be better not to read them at all. They need to be read over and over again and given constant thought and attention. They relate quite ordinary, everyday events which point to another world, and they offer their judgments in a spirit of innocence—judgments whose import only becomes clear in the inexhaustible range of connection between them. In an undertone and in a roundabout way they give voice to the unutterable, and the manner in which they are whispered forth, as it were, is profoundly akin to the language of the Bible translation.

Yet the utterances of Chassidism do not recall those of a universalistic religion. They are not comprehensible apart from a background of Talmud and Kabbala. The Chassidim were not primarily Talmudic scholars who spent their days in learning and devoted themselves to intellectual disputation in which, instance by instance, understanding and memory were put to the test; however, they were nonetheless at home with the Talmud and were steeped in its whole world of ideas. They had, moreover, felt the influence of the Kabbala, the often disjointed and singular wisdom of which was gathered up in the book of *Zohar*. The astounding thing about Chassidism is that despite these testators— never actually repudiated—a living kind of piety began to flourish which was neither engulfed in the ocean of the Talmud nor lost in the maze of the Kabbala. This was due to the strong personality of the *tsaddikim*.

We might translate the word *tsaddikim* as "righteous ones", but in so doing we must not forget that *tsaddik* became a title for the leader of a Chassidic congregation. In the earliest period he owed this unsolicited function to a charismatic gift recognized by those around him. In the period of decline there appeared the dynasties of tsaddikim who maintained what was basically a royal court and allowed themselves to be venerated as priest-princes. They were the guardians of fixed traditions, but they imparted no further impetus to religious life.

The first attempt to disseminate an account of Chassidic piety was made by Martin Buber with *Die Geschichten des Rabbi Nachman* (*The Tales of Rabbi Nachman*), which was published in 1906. In 1908 there followed *Die Legende des Baalschem* (*The Legend of the Baal Shem*) and in 1922 *Der grosse Maggid und seine Nachfolge* (*The Great Maggid and His Succession*). A good summary and a new introduction may be found in *Die Erzählungen der Chassidim* (*The Tales of the Chassidim*), published by Manesse Verlag in Zurich in 1949. For a fair assessment of all these reinterpretations it has to be stated emphatically from the start that Buber's approach to the sources is not that of the specialist scholar. Buber is proclaiming and passing on what has been spoken to him and has set him on a new trail. We are looking into the face of Chassidism as Buber beheld it.

In this way we are initiated into the circle of the Chassidim who relate the stories of their Tsaddikim. This story telling is an event marked with the solemnity of a sacred rite. Thus a shaft of light was seen to ascend from the room in which the devout were sitting while they recounted the deeds of their predecessors. As they uttered their stories, they were suffused with the primeval divine light, the marvels performed by the Tsaddikim became a reality once again, and the power of their words and of their actions was shed abroad. The account of a miraculous cure may have a curative effect. An old man, a paralytic, who is speaking to his grandson of the Baal Shem Tov, is seized with rapture when he describes the ecstatic dance of his Tsaddik. As he speaks he goes through the steps of the dance and is cured of his paralysis because he has told the story so well—that is, in such a way that it serves to help him.

The stories recounted by the Chassidim deal with ordinary events which have become extraordinary because they serve to express the meaning of existence. They describe actions that are transposed into liberating maxims; they give answers to questions which, once they have been raised, assume a scope far beyond the purpose or expectation of the questioner.

During a conference at Bentveld in 1947 Buber spoke on the subject of "Der Weg des Menschen nach der chassidischen Lehre," ("The Way for Man according to Chassidic Teaching") and took as his starting point a story told of Rabbi Shnever Salman, who was thrown into jail and there fell into conversation with a commissioner of police. The latter faced him with the problem of how an omniscient God could ask the question: "Where art thou?" When the commissioner of police expressed his belief that Holy Writ is perennial and that it enfolds within itself every age, generation and individual, the tsaddik said: "Well now, in every age God calls to every person; where are you in your world? So many days and years of your allotted span have passed—what in that time have you achieved in your world?

That, more or less, is how God speaks; for forty-six years you have lived, and what are you now?" When the commissioner of police heard his age given so precisely, he put on a bold front, clapped his hand on the rabbi's shoulder and exclaimed "Bravo!" —but in his heart he trembled. Here we have an example of a personal answer being given to a bogus question. The question affords an opening for the confrontation of an individual with himself. From the question has emerged an answer of profound import. Thus the tsaddik is there to give help and not to be any kind of substitute. He needs the congregation to be around him and the questioner to address him; although he draws strength from solitude, as a mere individual he is unproductive.

The very recollection of the first and greatest of the tsaddikim has about it something almost uncanny, like the encounter with the holy. What is related of them is not susceptible of being checked for its reliability as history, but in the testimony of inspired souls they are present and real enough. Israel ben Eliëzer of Mesbiz (1700-1760) acquired the further name of Baal Shem Tov (he who possesses the name of God) and also "a good name" —that is, one designating a confidential representative. His successor was Rabbi Dow Bär (d. 1772), whose sobriquet was "the great maggid" (propounder) of Mesritsch. He had three hundred disciples who met their deaths during the period of the Polish struggle for liberation and the Napoleonic Wars, which were taken to be the wars of Gog and Magog. The big question, then, is what it was in their lives and in their words which spoke so compellingly to Buber that it speaks also to us.

They did not come along with any specific creed or with an infallible authority. Although each tsaddik was accepted among his pupils as though he were the messiah, it was held to be idolatry for anyone to regard his rabbi as the only true one. The secret of their influence is to be sought first and foremost in the humble spirit in which they shared the life of their fellows, participating in their confusion and their sorrows, their ignorance and sin. They never set themselves up on a pedestal, but lived and moved among the people, all of whom, as they believed, carried within them a spark of the divine fire. They made themselves adjustable, just as the father who adjusts himself to his inquisitive child mirrors the self-abasement of God in his concern for the well-being of his creatures. Humility in Hebrew is *shiphlut*. It is a mark of the true mystic in his relationship toward other men. *Shiphlut* ensures that he never sets himself over against someone else in a hostile or competitive spirit, but rather sees himself as the other and sees the other in himself. In this way one can even put oneself in the place of things and animals; thus it is said of Baal Shem Tov that he conversed with the beasts.

In his interpretation of Chassidism Buber placed great emphasis on its ability to heal the breach between matter and spirit, between the profane and the holy, between God and the world. He returns again and again in his synthesis of Chassidic ideas and insights to the theme of the reunification of what in the creation was one and has since disintegrated. In ecstasy the human being can obtain release from the finite world and even from himself. The Chassidic equivalent for "ecstasy" is *hithlahavut*, a word whose root signifies "kindle" or "inflame". Such ecstasy uplifts prayers to God and issues in service, in *avodah*. This service is not only obedience to the rules prescribed by tradition but can also find its expression in each and every profane action. The important thing, therefore, is not only that the food regulations be observed but also that in the act of eating one should be grateful to God and should esteem him as the giver of all things. Thus the man of piety, by eating in a spirit of joy, can be God's co-worker and can make his contribution to the *yichud*, the process of reunifying, which cancels out the wretched consequences of division. But eating and drinking in this way is possible only to the person who, in all that he does or does not do, seeks in mind and heart to achieve the world's redemption. This quality of purposiveness is the *kawwanah*, which in the Talmud accompanies prayer but in Chassidic circles is envisaged as the highly charged intention that can elevate every profane action to the sphere of the holy.

Therefore, what Buber found in Chassidism was a distinctly positive evaluation of the world with all its good and evil, sorrow and sin. The realities of life were accepted, asceticism and melancholy were repudiated, and joy in life was seen as a mark of divine illumination.

What made it possible for Buber to pass on in such a one-sided fashion what was indeed in many respects an emancipating message was that the tsaddikim, generally speaking, were not given to wasting words. This has been pointed out in a penetrating essay by Riwka Schatz-Uffênheimer, entitled "Die Stellung des Menschen zu Gott und Welt in Buber's Darstellung des Chassidismus" ("Man's Bearing toward God and the World in Buber's Version of Chassidism"), which was included in the volume *Martin Buber*, published by P. A. Schilpp and M. Riedman (Stuttgart, 1963, pp. 275-302). She cites an example that has to do with the value attached to joy. There is a well-known dictum of a certain tsaddik in which a sinner is commended because he never allows repentance or remorse to depress him but always remains bright and cheerful. Now when a traditional saying of this sort is read completely out of context, one may draw the false conclusion that in Chassidic circles joy was not only elevated to the status of a supreme good, religiously speaking, but was also thought of as securing satisfaction for sins. That is simply not so. If and when feelings of sadness and a somber frame of mind are condemned, it is for a very particular reason: they distract an individual from his goal, throwing him back onto himself and onto preoccupation with himself—and that impedes his living with God and with his fellow man.

It is very much a question whether Chassidism says "yes" to the world quite as positively as Buber would have us believe. Certainly its devotees were not ascetic, but still they kept aloof to some extent from the profane activities that permit life to be what it is. The tsaddik ate and drank, lived with a woman, carried on his work as a lumber merchant or a chemist and entered into all activities of life. Whatever people did they did in concentration on the divine element secretly present in all things, but that is not to say that in itself eating or drinking was drawn out of the profane sphere or that any new appreciation of woman had emerged. Woman remained a means to living and to living with God—as did eating and drinking—and when it is said of Shalom of Belz that he would appear with his wife and keep her at his side so that they were "like Adam and Eve in paradise", this is not intended as a message to indicate the absolute character of the cohabitation of man and wife. The woman's place is as a means to the service of God, and it is from this circumstance that she derives her lofty status and dignity.

The legends that have been handed down to us do not give us any adequate idea of the extent to which the tsaddik, with his circle of pupils, his congregation and those who happened to pass before him, wrestled with the problems of the meaning of existence and the ground of the world's being. Each day these pious ones were tried and tested when they sought after God in prayer, and the world set itself in opposition to them or, as subsequently happened, persecuted them.

A searching critical appraisal of the picture that Buber has drawn of Chassidism has been put forward by the greatest authority on Jewish mysticism now living, Professor Gershom Scholem. He has voiced this appraisal, for example, in two articles which, under the title "Martin Bubers Deutung des Chassidismus" ("Martin Buber's Interpretation of Chassidism"), first appeared in *Neue Züricher Zeitung* (May 20 and 27, 1962) and were reprinted in the volume *Judaica* (Frankfurt am Main, 1963), pp. 165-206. This learned author is one of the few people who not only have access to the sources but also have employed a systematic method of editing and arranging them. With regard to his respect for Buber's achievement, he argues that in the latter's Chassidic writings the true face of Chassidism is not revealed to us.

Chassidism in its prime was rooted in the Kabbala, possessed all the characteristics of Gnosticism and was esoteric. In that respect it evinced elements that Buber could not assimilate, simply because—by his own admission—he was unable to comprehend them. In what he passed on, therefore, he restricted himself to legends, epigrams and anecdotes of the Chassidic saints, avoiding the literature of theorizing. He was aware of this imbalance, but defended it with arguments that are scarcely tenable when measured by scientific standards. He took the theoretical literature to be a commentary on the text proper, which had itself been preserved in the legend. The commentary gave only the theory, but the legend stood for the living reality. Scholem utters a forceful protest at this arbitrary division between theory and "real life". He argues that the stories are the forms into which have been cast the ideas discoverable in the theoretical writings half a century before. And those are the ideas of the Gnostics, of the Kabbala, which in the form presented amount to this: sparks of the divine light and life are dispersed all over the world, as in a kind of exile. They yearn intensely to be restored through the actions of human beings to their original place in the divine harmony of all being.

The hub of the ideas implicit in this view is the expression in Proverbs 3, 6: "Know him in all your ways." This is to say that there is no line of separation between the Torah and the profane sphere of life. It also means that in this mundane state of things there exists nothing, great or small, of which we can say that it does not concern God. The *yichudim*—that is, "the acts of reunification", can occur anywhere: in the marketplace and in conversation about politics, in the coming together of a man and a woman and during the process of instruction. All this Buber heartily endorses and proclaims, but the sequel—and that is the essential thing—he passes over in silence. The essential point is that the "reunifying", which in prayer and contemplation may be attained at any time and in any place, does away with the reality of the "here and now". The eternal oneness and presence of transcendence does not imply that one can proceed to affirm the concrete and the reality of time and space. The encounter with the divine in the common things of life is a kind of springboard into another, higher world. At this juncture Chassidism surrenders something of the fascination which the singular, the exceptional, exerts, and as a type of devotion and piety it is on much the same footing as the mysticism to be encountered in other religions as well. Be that as it may, it is thus, and not otherwise, that the texts oblige us to view it. Scholem makes this quite clear from the following example:

R. Wolf of Shitomir says that the Baalshem once asked an eminent scholar how he stood with regard to prayer: "How do you behave and on what do you focus your thoughts during prayer?" He answered: "I link myself with everything that is present within the whole created order in the way of individual vitality. For in everything that is created—and in each thing individually—there must be a vital force flowing into it from the plenitude of the Godhead. I link myself to them when I address my words to God, so as to penetrate with my prayer into the highest regions." The Baalshem said to him: "In so doing you devastate the world, for while you extract its vital force and raise it above, each created thing considered individually is left without its vitality." He said to him: "But then how can I, so long as I am linking myself with them, extract their vital force?" The Baalshem replied: "From what you say your prayer cannot carry much weight, since you do not credit yourself with the power to extract their vital force from them and raise it on high."

This dialogue, Scholem says, might well be taken as a conversation between the Baalshem and Buber. Prayer is an esoteric act which the true expert alone can perform. Its ultimate effect is not to realize the concrete in its concreteness. The absorption of the person at prayer voids the concrete and does not fill his mind with concrete things.

It is not true to say that in what Chassidism has to tell us the division between "life in God" and "life in the world"—what Buber described as the original sin of every religion—is surmounted in a concrete unity. Life in the world ceases to be a life in the world, if and when in contemplation its divine roots are disclosed and life is turned into a life in God.

But it has not been our task to write either about the beginnings of Chassidism or its decadence. Our present concern is only the actual religious phenomenon evoked by Buber which he claimed to be the fruit of his encounter with Chassidism. We are ready to agree with him that in Baal Shem Tov and the great Maggid we are brought face to face with one of the most powerful manifestations of a vital and seminal quality of faith. In them flowers once again the resolute proclivity of the Jew to serve God in the world and to consecrate the diurnal course of living to the Holy One.

Chassidism as Buber presents it to us affirms the high estate and humble estate of man in two juxtaposed sayings of Rabbi Bunam: "For my sake is man created" and "I am dust and ashes." It teaches him to be content with his place and with the possibilities afforded him, as Rabbi Susha states: "In the world to come I shall not be asked: 'Why were you no Moses?' But I shall be asked: 'Why were you no Susha?' " The fulfillment of existence is to be found in the place where we are. It was in vain that Rabbi Eisik journeyed from Cracow to Prague to find the treasure that lay hidden at home beneath his hearth. But above all, the Chassidism which Buber delivers to us is the news of a divine grace and favor that offers man the suprahuman opportunity to collaborate in God's coming to the world.

Man and Men

Man is the creature who, being what he is, makes that very being his concern. Heidegger's[1] formula points to a relation of man to himself—an interrogative relation. The most ancient texts we know corroborate this view: man is the creature who asks about himself. Admittedly, he also asks about the world around him, about Physis (nature), about Arché (the beginning) and about the gods, but in these questions—and indeed with them— he asks also about himself: "What is man...?" (Ps. 8, 5).

There are times, however, when the question which man poses about himself assumes a note of special urgency, because man experiences his situation as man with a new and greater intensity, as setting him apart from the world, as alienating him from it, thrusting him out from the nexus, the solidarity, of things as a whole. Such times are the great periods of anthropology—and ours is such a time.

The Anthropological Issue

It hardly needs to be said that Martin Buber pondered deeply upon man and wrote about him too, as witness not only the indeed somewhat earlier but still celebrated books *Ich und Du* (1923: *Werke* I: 77-170) and *Zwiesprache* (1930: *Werke* I: 171-214) which effected a considerable change in European philosophy—one could certainly argue that up to this point idealism was not fully and finally routed—but also his later works, the book which came out in 1943, entitled *Baayath ha-adam* (= *Das Problem des Menschen*) (*Werke* I: 307-408), and the articles in *Studia Philosophica* and other journals, now collected under the title *Beiträge zu einer philosophischen Anthropologie* (Werke I:

---

[1] Martin Heidegger, *Sein und Zeit* I (Halle, [5] 1941), 12: " 'Being present' ... is distinguished ontically by the fact that this being concerns itself in its being with that very being."

409-502). I also have in mind the many articles, brochures and so on which Buber devoted to the subject of education and which, at least indirectly, are a contribution to anthropology. And finally, does not the fondness for Chassidism also go hand in hand with what is said regarding man by the pious men of Jewry? The little book called *Der Weg des Menschen nach der chassidischen Lehre* (*Werke* III: 713-38) makes that at least probable.

What Buber has written about man certainly does not amount to a systematically elaborated anthropology. He made certain contributions, nothing more. Any comprehensive anthropology would be bound to deal with issues on which Buber has nothing to say. Moreover, in what he does contribute he restricts himself to a fairly narrow range of subject matter. Yet that is precisely what makes his work so important. What he wrote regarding "man's being as dialogue" is a vital contribution to thought on the X which we are. Buber wants to place himself against all loose and vague ideas and all show of "philosophic" profundity; he wants to avoid commitment to one particular program and simply to write about man as he really is—that is, about man in his close and binding relation with a world, with his fellowmen and with God, the eternal Thou: "I speak of nothing other than man as he really is, of you and me, of our life and our world—not of an I-in-itself and not of Being-in-itself" (*Werke* I: 86). That was written in 1923. Many years later, in *Baayath ha-adam*, Buber says the same thing. Kant's question "What is man?" can only be answered if our starting point is man—man living in the world, man in his relations to all that is. "Only man, who actualizes with his whole being . . . the relations possible to him, can help us really and truly to know what man is" (*Werke* I: 400). Our concern, then, is with this *actual* man, and we shall see that both idealism and existentialism pass him by.

To ask about man is to ask about the *Prinzip des Menschseins;* it is to ask what constitutes "being human" and what distinguishes that, for instance, from the "being" of sun and moon, stars, animals and implements. What is the category of being, of existing, that goes by the name of man? That *Prinzip*, Martin Buber says, is a twofold relation to the world or, rather, a twofold motion:[2] away from the world and back to the world:

[2] Buber, *Die Geschichte des dialogischen Prinzips* (*The History of the Dialogical Principle*) (*Werke* I:291-305).

Urdistanzierung, In-Beziehungtreten (primary or initial self-distancing and entering into relation). Along with many other anthropologists of our day Buber starts from the fundamental distinction between man and animal, as enunciated by scholars such as von Uexkuell. The animal has a world around it in which it perceives and discerns what it needs to conserve and continue its life: the so-called *Merk-Welt.* This whole world—as yet the question of a world does not, strictly speaking, arise—is pure presence, into which the animal enters and within which it is engrossed. The world here is never simply given, never simply at hand, but always *aktions-relativ,* always related to the *Aktionsplan* of the animal, of whatever species; and here we must observe that this "plan" is not based on choice or deliberation, but rather is something given with the animal's sensory organization. We might say that there is no area of "play", no give and take, between the animal and its world. Indeed we could go further and say that there is even no "between". In this world there are no things, no objects; there are only signals, stimuli, and the animal "responds", without option, with its actions. It cannot distance itself.

This, then, is the *Prinzip des Menschseins:* that man has the ability to distance himself, to stand off from his world, and that through this a "world" comes into being. To put it quite simply: the fly that alights on a painting notices whatever serves its purpose, whereas a human being sees it "as a whole". It is worth considering whether Buber is not right when he relates man and world to each other in such a way that only with man, who distances himself from his *Merk-Welt* (which he also has), does a world arise as something self-subsistent over against him. There is a strong case, therefore, for following the distinction that he makes: the animal has its *Bereich* (its proper sphere), but the human being has a world. In *Baayath ha-adam* Buber calls this the basic fact of anthropology and the most odd of all mundane facts: "There is in the world a being that knows a world *qua* world . . . and knows himself as one who is cognizant of this knowing" (*Werke* I:351). There is as much reason here to speak, as Pascal does, of the stature of man, who is more than the entire world *parce qu'il sait,* as to assert with Anthonie Donker that man has become a stranger in the world:

a stranger to the shell and fire
to tendril and wild rose . . .

If this is the first motion that constitutes "being-as-man"—the distancing of oneself from the world, the *Urdistanzierung* in virtue of which the world begins to be world—there is also a second motion: one back to the world, the *In-Beziehungtreten*. It should be observed at this point that logically the first motion does in fact precede the second—for only the being that has marked itself off from its world can have a relation, a *Beziehung*, to its world—but that they are not separable in time. There is never distance alone, but always the one thing and the other: distance and *Beziehung*. It is with this second motion that history begins. In the first motion "being-as-man" is rendered possible; in the second it is actualized. In Buber's own words: "The act of self-distancing produces the human situation; the *Beziehung* initiates the process of becoming human in that situation" (*Werke* I: 416). Thus the process itself—and that lies behind what we have heard about the "real man"—takes place in history, in the relations within which man sets himself or which he himself creates. That is why anyone who in his anthropological thinking dissociates man from his relationships ends up by losing sight of man as he really is.

All this implies the rejection of idealism, which starts, surely, with the *Ich-an-sich*, the I-in-itself, and with the *Sein-an-sich*, being-in-itself, and then goes on to inquire about the relation of this "unreal" I to being, to the world and so forth, and by asking in that way shuts itself off from access to the real man. "There is no *Ich-an-sich*" (*Werke* I:79). With that brief sentence Buber makes his defense against the philosophical monologue which extends from Plato to Nietzsche, for even one who, like Plato, composes dialogues is still capable of thinking in monologue.

Man in His Relationships

The philosophy of human relationships, of "being-as-man" *qua* dialogue, must start with a fundamental distinction. Man stands in another relation to things, the objects that he uses, the implements that he handles, than to people and to God. In the first situation he is dealing with an *Es*/It, in the second with a *Du*/ Thou. At the outset of his short book *Ich und Du* Buber introduces this distinction, one that recurs throughout his works: "To man the world is twofold, in accordance with his twofold attitude. The attitude of man is twofold, in accordance with the twofold nature of the primary words which he speaks. The primary words are not isolated words, but combined words. The one primary word is the combination *I-Thou*. The other primary word is the combination *I-It*, wherein, without a change in the primary word, one of the words *He* and *She* can replace *It*. Hence the *I* of man is also twofold, for the I of the primary word *I-Thou* is a different *I* from that of the primary word *I-It*" (*I and Thou*, tr. R. Gregor Smith: Edinburgh, 1937, p. 3; *Werke* I: 79).[3] A little later on comes the sentence, part of which has been quoted already: "There is no *I* taken in itself, but only the *I* of the primary word *I-Thou* and the *I* of the primary word *I-It*" (*I and Thou*, p. 4; *Werke* I:79).

It is essential to pause for a moment over these opening sentences of a book which in the Europe of 1923 came as a revelation. "Primary word" (Dutch: *grond-woord*) here renders the German *Grundwort*—a term that one would suppose to have been just as novel and as strange as *grond-woord* is in Dutch. There are times when a thinker has to create neologisms if there is something new to be said, and in such a case that is not wilfullness but a necessity. *Grundwort* contains an echo of *gründen*, *begründen* (to found, to establish). The word that I utter, insofar as it is a primary word, is not one in which relations or situations already present are repeated and expressed; the word *gründet* constitutes the relation in which I stand to It—or to you (thee),

---

[3] Because these opening sentences of *Ich und Du* are of such great importance for the further understanding of Buber's thought, we give here the German text: "Die Welt ist dem Menschen zwiefältig nach seiner zwiefältigen Haltung. Die Haltung des Menschen ist zwiefältig nach der Zwiefalt der Grundworte, die er sprechen kann. Die Grundworte sind nicht Einzelworte, sondern Wortpaare. Das eine Grundwort ist das Wortpaar Ich-Du. Das andere Grundwort ist das Grundwort Ich-Es:wobei, ohne Änderung des Grundwortes, für Es auch eins der Worte Er und Sie eintreten kann. Somit ist auch das Ich des Menschen zwiefältig. Denn das Ich des Grundworts Ich-Du ist ein andres als das des Grundworts Ich-Es."

the one or the other. I determine in which realm I am situated: "I
perceive something. . . . I will something. . . . I think something.
. . .This and the like together establish (*gründet*) the realm of It.
But the realm of Thou has a different basis" (*I and Thou*, p. 4;
Werke I:80). Is there implicit in this way of talking about man
in terms of establishing and projecting a world, of constituting a
world, some recollection of Genesis 1? Or is it a continuation—
an indeed fundamentally altered, yet in its modified formulation,
still recognizable continuation—of idealism? The former is more
likely—and yet it is a question whether man himself, with his
primary word, *establishes* his relationships. That may be true of
the It-world, but does it also hold good of the world in which
you encounter me? Can a man utter the authoritative word (the
primary word) by which the other becomes You (Thou) for
him? Can a man evoke this world and determine its boundaries?
At all events we read very early in *Ich und Du*: "The *Thou*
meets me through grace—it is not found by seeking" (*I and
Thou*, p. 11; *Werke* I:85). In other words, it is not within my
power to cause another to become Thou for me. Buber then adds:
"But my speaking of the primary word to it is an act of my being"
I and Thou, p. 11; *Werke* I:85). That much may be true, but if
he really means what he said earlier—if it is indeed through grace
that the Thou meets me—then it can no longer be maintained
that it is I who speak the primary word, that it is I who do the
establishing. That is evident enough in the relation of a man to
the human Thou, but still more so in the relation of a human
being to God. It is surely not the human being who brings about,
who *establishes*, a relation to the eternal Thou! It is through
grace that Thou does meet me. A man may seek, but "it is not to
be found by seeking". A man may ask:

Oh DU,	O Thou,
nimmer bleibe fern!	be never far absent from me!
Du mein Wesensstand	Thou who art the condition of my being,
zu meiner Hilfe eile!	Make haste to help me!

But *establishing* is what he cannot do.

Ich und Du is an endeavor to describe the "structure" of the
two worlds in which man participates: the It-world and the

Thou-world. When schematized, the contrast between them can be set out in this way:[4]

I—It	I—Thou
Experience (i.e., practice, expertise)	Relation
Object	Presence
Utilizing	Encounter
Provision for, or attention to	Love
Fate	Fortune, (appointed) destiny
Discretion, caprice or arbitrary will	Freedom
Having	Being

It would be possible, of course, to enlarge the "table of categories" on both sides, but that is unnecessary. The essential cate-

---

[4] There are good reasons why most of the categories listed here should be given in German, for we are now dealing with concepts that are of fundamental import for giving an account of these two worlds, and a translation is seldom—particularly when it comes to "isolated" words—entirely adequate. For instance, it would be quite possible to translate the word *Begegnung* as "encounter" or "meeting"—indeed, that is just what the dictionary says—but the link between *Gegenwart* and *Begegnung* (both contain the element *gegen*) is bound in that way to be obscured. The necessity for letting the German words stand is most pressing in the case of *Verhängnis* in the first list and *Schicksal* in the second. We are bound to translate the former as "fate", and likewise the latter. At best, we might differentiate by rendering one of the two with the word "fatum". But for Buber it is a matter of two worlds: where there is *Verhängnis* there can be no *Schicksal*, and vice versa. *Verhängnis* is what befalls me, adventitiously and unforeseen; it cuts across my having and using of the world, and sets bounds to the exercise of my will. It should not be so, but it is so. I have to give way to it to accommodate myself, but this facticity, this "it is so", lends no meaning to my life. *Verhängnis* and "doing what I will" are opposed. I try to evade *Verhängnis*—and it overtakes me. With *Schicksal* things are different. It is equally unforeseen, but it is not fortuitous. It "has to be so". There is no opposition, therefore, between *Schicksal* and freedom—quite the contrary. What has confronted me as *Schicksal*, though unforeseen, is the working out of my freedom. The meaning of my life, the "one thing needful", all at once becomes visible, and I do not resign or reconcile myself, but assent to what has fallen to my lot. Thus for Paul Tillich freedom and *destiny* are bound up with each other; cf. P. Tillich: *Systematic Theology* I (London, 1953), pp. 201-06. Thus too for Karl Jaspers freedom and necessity coincide in *müssen* (being obligated [by duty] to . . .), which is perfect freedom; cf. Karl Jaspers: *Philosophie* (Berlin-Göttingen-Heidelberg,[2] 1948) pp. 462-63. In the same way Friedrich Nietzsche speaks about *Amor Fati*. While *Verhängnis*, therefore, is an alien power, *Schicksal* is my real, my proper condition. Whereas *Verhängnis* is speechless—it was "dumb chance"—my *Schicksal* is a question addressed to me, and at the same time my answer to that question. Now my life has become wholly real.

gories are here already. It is evident, then, that in the realm where
"thou" and "I" are conjoined there is no "experience" (*savoir-faire*); it is a "thingless" realm, a realm without "having" and
without arbitrariness, where you (thou) are not put to use.
"Thou" and "I" are in a relation of love, which has no goal or
purpose beyond itself, and in a relation of freedom, which is
apprehended as a kind of destiny (*Schicksal*)—and these are not
opposites here! We simply *are*—and it *has* to be like this. Con-
versely, the world of I and It is a world of "experience" (exper-
tise), in which I utilize things, manage and regulate, have "as a
means to" some goal. Even if a person should come within this
world—and that may indeed be the case: "Without a change in
the primary word, one of the words *He* and *She* can replace *It*" (*I
and Thou*, p. 3; *Werke* I:70)—he is there only as an object of my
attention, as an object of my disdain, as a man whom I can use or
who should not get in my way, and so forth, but no love exists
between us. Should that occur (and it always may!), the It-
world, the world of "having" and "using", the realm of the
capricious will, is at once left behind, and then we *are*, are together, in the fragile realm of freedom.

A man lives by dint of things; he alters, uses, regulates, *has*
them, and even he or she is a thing for me, a "person-thing",
whom I have at my disposal. "Je serai ton esclave et ta chose,"
says Electra to Jupiter in one of Sartre's plays,[5] and that is the
perfect expression for what occurs here. The person is no longer
a person to me, but some sort of thing. He is mine to manipulate,
and I am as solitary as he. "And in all the seriousness of truth,
hear this: without *It* man cannot live. But he who lives with *It*
alone is not a man" (*I and Thou*, p. 34; *Werke* I:101). "He is a
man who concerns himself with man in such a way that for him
the self (your self!) is fully involved. Men become 'man' together—or else not at all, and in that case they never really begin
to live" (*Werke* I:368). "I become through my relation to the
Thou; as I become *I*, I say *Thou*" (*I and Thou*, p. 11; *Werke*
I:85).

Those are the two worlds. The one is static, substantial, con-
tinuous, invariably there: the world of it and it, and it and he,
and he and she, and she and it. I perceive something, I think

[5] J-P. Sartre, *Théâtre* (Paris,[48] 1947), p. 104.

something, I will something. This is the end in view; the means are perfect: I-It. The other world is puny, fragile, discontinuous and all too often non-existent, not to be commanded at will or held in one's grasp. You become he again for me. ". . . every *Thou* in our world must become an It . . . an object among objects—perhaps the chief object, but still one of them, fixed in its size and its limits. . . . The human being who was even now single and unconditioned, not something lying at hand, only present, not able to be experienced . . . has now become again a *He* or a *She*" (*I and Thou*, pp. 16-17; *Werke* I:89). This second world may be the real world, the world in which a man comes to be a human being, but how can it subsist in the State, in industry, in the economic realm? "The human use of human beings", ideologizing, imbuing men with a spirit of fanaticism, Labor Day parades, a solution to the Jewish question—the world of the human being ceases to be.

As the centuries have passed, the It-world has grown larger and larger, while the Thou-world has been forced further and further back. The one process is a consequence of the other, for "the development of the ability to experience and use comes about mostly through the decrease of man's power to enter into relation" (*I and Thou*, pp. 38-39; *Werke* I:103). In the end it comes very much to look as though only one primary word is left: I-It. When that happens, being-as-man is then eventually absorbed— to use Heidegger's expression—in *Steuerung und Sicherung* ("pilotage and safety-first").

The world that then emerges has order and permanence and continuity. It is a world that you can manage and manipulate as you will, one in which you can feel "at home". Is not that the real world? And is not all the talk about I-thou so much wild and nebulous fantasy when set beside the real world? Are those moments when I encounter a human being—and encounter him in such a way that he becomes a thou—anything more than lyrical and dramatic episodes, splendid, of course, and undoubtedly fascinating, but still episodes which, *unheimlich* as they are, undermine security and the sense of being on easy terms with the world? Are we still ready to risk meeting the other in a real encounter, to involve ourselves in his "presence"? If so, are we still able to do it? Is our ability to be not crowded out by our longing to have? These questions touch on those that Heidegger raises in his later writings—for instance, in his article "Die Frage nach der Technik," (The Problem of Technics").[6]

There is in *Ich und Du* an element of the prophetic. Here is a prophet lifting up his voice in the wilderness of the It-world, in which man misses his way. Can we say, forty years later, that Buber took too somber a view, that we know very well that the It-world has a greater measure of order, of stability and continuity, than the world which we experience as grace, where the primary word I-thou is spoken, but that nevertheless we proceed on the basis that this latter world is "more real" and is essential to being-as-man? Can we say that we are doing everything we can to keep room for this world within the *Gestell* (M. Heidegger), the "structure", in which we are embroiled, so that a man can live as a human being? Whatever the reason, Buber states: "In all the seriousness of truth, hear this: without *It* man cannot live. But he who lives with *It* alone is not a man" (*I and Thou*, p. 34; *Werke* I:101). But how can we live?

Is it by sheer chance that both Heidegger and Buber express a final and unfounded confidence—that is, one not founded upon any apprehendable certitude—by citing the words of Hölderlin:

Wo aber Gefahr ist, wächst   Yet where danger is, there
das Rettende auch. . . .[7]   arises also a means of rescue. . . .

Where the danger lies we have already seen: it lies in the growth of the It-world in the state, in technics and so forth. But what is the remedial factor, and where are we to find it? More about that presently—but let it be said here that we shall find ourselves in the presence of such words as sacrifice and grace and faith: words belonging to the world of religion, which is not a world alongside or behind the "real" world. In the language of the prophets, the saving factor resides in the *teshuwah*, the "turning point", which man cannot accomplish for himself but must indeed desiderate. "The matter will not turn out according to his decision, but what is to come will come only when he decides on

[6] M. Heidegger, "Die Frage nach der Technik," in *Vortraege und Aufsaetze* (Pfullingen, 1954), pp. 13-44, especially pp. 27ff.
[7] M. Heidegger, *Vortraege und Aufsaetze*, pp. 36ff.

what he is able to will" (*I and Thou*, p. 59; *Werke* I:118). Man must take the risk of contemplating the unrealized, of reflecting upon the real I; he must venture to despair of what life in the world has become—and venture also to take his leave of that misguided urge to uphold the self, which makes him seek refuge in "having things". And beyond that, as Hamlet says the readiness is all.

Heidegger Criticized

We have seen that because of his philosophy of "being-*qua*-man" as dialogue, Buber's thinking breaks through and dismantles idealism. With the same starting point as a basis, he moves to an attack on existentialism, and specifically on Heidegger. In *Ich und Du* there is not a word said about existentialism, simply because that little book came out four years in advance of *Sein und Zeit* I. In *Baayath ha-adam*, however, Buber deals at some length with Heidegger (*Werke* I:360-80). Anybody familiar with what is said in *Sein und Zeit* I about *Dasein*—that is, about "being-as-man"—will not be surprised at Buber's rejection of Heidegger's analysis of the term. Heidegger rightly says that the individual, if he is to find himself and attain to an authentic existence, must escape from the powerful hold which "they" have over him—"they" here being all and sundry who prescribe for me what I should want, what I am to think, what I must do and what I have to be. And Heidegger rightly locates man in his world, describing *Dasein* as an *in-der-Welt-Sein* (a "being-in-the-world"), which is at the same time a *Mitsein*, a "being-together-with-others". But for Heidegger this no more amounts to an I-thou relationship than it does for Jean-Paul Sartre, who has little more to say of other people than that "they are my hell".[8]

The truth is that for Heidegger the supreme factor in human relations is not love—that is out of the question—but *Fürsorge*, "concern", "attention", with, of course, its deficient variants (*modi*)—for instance, indifference. *Fürsorge*, however, is already included by Buber in *Ich und Du*—and thus prior to the publication of *Sein und Zeit* I—among the categories of the It-world,

[8] J-P. Sartre, op. cit., p. 167.

and he says there (did Heidegger perhaps read this?) that to do violence to people, provided they are encountered as human beings, is always preferable to a wraithlike *Fürsorge* for so many faceless numbers. In the first situation there at least remains a way to God, whereas in the second everything ends in Nothingness (*I and Thou*, p. 24; *Werke* I:94). When attacking Heidegger in *Baayath ha-adam* Buber says basically the same thing: "Heidegger's *Dasein* is a monologue. The man characterized by *Dasein*, in Heidegger's sense, or by that *Selbstsein* ('being-the-self') which according to Heidegger is the goal of existence, is not man in a living rapport with man; rather, this is the man who cannot live with man but can only recognize a 'real' mode of living in intercourse with himself. That, however, is no more than an empty shadow of real living" (*Werke* I:365). And as regards Heidegger's *Fürsorge*, he says: "In such concern—if it is not also something more than that—man remains essentially on his own, even when impelled by the strongest feelings of compassion. He inclines toward the other in actively assisting him, but the frontiers of his own being are not broken through. He does not open his own *self* to the other, but gives him his help; nor does he look for any reciprocity—indeed, he does not want it. He unites with, responds to, the other person, as we say, but he does not at all wish that other person to respond to him. To be truly related, on the other hand, means that the frontiers of my being are actually broken through" (*Werke* I:368). With Heidegger's man this is not so: "With Heidegger the self is a closed system" (*Werke* I:369); "In Heidegger's world there is no Thou . . . no Thou really spoken with the whole of one's being" (*Werke* I:370).

It is a moot point whether this attack also finds a target in the later Heidegger, the Heidegger of *Holzwege* (*False Paths*), of *Vortraege und Aufsaetze* (*Lectures and Essays*), and so forth—books which had not yet appeared when Buber wrote *Baayath ha-adam*. Do not the *Sterbliche* in these pages—the mortal beings on their road to death—come closer to Buber's I-Thou than was the case in *Sein und Zeit* I? But there is a question that is still more to the point. Is not what Buber says about "fundamental relationships" (*Beziehungen*)—those in which a man comes to be a human being—a string of gratuitous assertions,—if indeed not simply daydreaming on the part of an enthusiast! How can love be a possibility? In what scheme, what theory of existence is it grounded? Buber has little to say on this score. In the matter of ontology *Ich und Du* and *Baayath ha-adam* lags far behind the work of Heidegger. There is in *Ich und Du*, however, a small clue, where Buber speaks of an "*a priori*" in the relationship—the term reminds us of Kant—which is given along with "being-as-man". He speaks here more in a poetic vein than in strictly ontological terms, but he does point in a direction that may be further explored. The fragment starts with a profound interpretation of Genesis 1, 1 and John 1, 1: "*Im Anfang ist die Beziehung: als Kategorie des Wesens, als Bereitschaft, fassende Form, Seelenmodell; das Apriori der Beziehung; das eingeborene Du. Die erlebten Beziehungen sind Realisierungen des eingeborenen Du am begegnenden*" ("In the beginning is relation—as category of being, readiness, grasping form, mold for the soul; it is the *a priori* of relation, *the inborn Thou*") (*I and Thou*, p. 27; *Werke* I:96). Encounter is possible because you are already "present" along with my "being-as man", and because I know myself to be in dependence on you.

This *a priori* aspect of relationship is also the ground of confidence in the *teshuwah* ("turning about") by which man is able to escape the encompassing danger. *Das eingeborene Du* (the inborn Thou) will not leave man alone; it is there even when he is absorbed in the business of "having" his world. It beckons him, and in so doing uncovers his estrangement. He may resist the call and pronounce it nothing but wild reverie, daydreaming—or he may heed it, and so set forth.

A Piece of History

In the history of European philosophy Buber was the first person to construct an anthropology consistently based on the motifs of dialogue and *Mitmenschlichkeit* (i.e., humanity-in-fellowship).

Buber himself saw certain initial approaches toward what he is saying in *Ich und Du* in some fragments of correspondence written by F. H. Jacobi (1743-1819). However, the real history of these themes begins only in the 19th century with the much maligned Ludwig Feuerbach (1804-1872) who, in taking his stand against the monologues of idealism, had discovered the *Notwendigkeit des Du für das Ich* (the I's essential need of the Thou), but then proceeded to misinterpret the meaning of this discovery when he went on to say specifically that the union, the oneness, of I and Thou is God. In this way the motif was given a "mystical" concept which is not to the point. Nonetheless, in *Baayath ha-adam* Buber gratefully acknowledges that it was Feuerbach who put him on the right track. After Feuerbach Buber refers to Sören Kierkegaard (1813-1855), the man who gave the word "existence" its modern meaning and also apprehended and described the relationship of man to God as an I-Thou relationship—but yet the man who thought it necessary, for the sake of this I-Thou relationship, to surrender all human relations that would entangle him in the realm of the finite.

For seventy years after Feuerbach and Kierkegaard nothing further transpired. A few echoes of the theme were heard, but nothing more was done to elaborate upon it. Was it that the theme as such offered so few possibilities, or were those possibilities it possessed a kind that failed to appeal to the 19th century? Whatever the reason, it was not until about 1920 that the Jewish thinkers Hermann Cohen and Franz Rosenzweig (whose *Stern der Erlösung* [*Star of Redemption*] appeared in 1921), together with the Roman Catholic, Ferdinand Ebner, took notice of it and set about putting it to use. Thus there was a remarkable coincidence of events round about the year 1920, for at that moment Buber was at work on his little book *Ich und Du*.

The names that we have mentioned here are part and parcel of the history of philosophy. More important, however, according to Martin Buber's own testimony, in bringing to birth *Ich und Du* was the contribution made by Chassidism. The principle of dialogue, even if it was not referred to in that way, was in fact the heart and center of Chassidic piety, as well as the real basis of every human relationship. Buber's study of Chassidism is not a self-contained aspect of his work alongside his philosophy and his study of the Old Testament. The unity of his work resides in the fact that his philosophy may be accurately described as "applied Chassidism".

God and Men

The Eternal Thou

Man lives by things. Man lives by the animals. Man lives by men. He lives in relations which are continually being disrupted; yet these relations must always be there, because "being man" perhaps we should say "becoming man"—is a matter of entering into relationship. For Buber every relationship is grounded in man's relationship to God, which like all genuine human relations is an I-Thou relation: not one of having and using—that is magic —but one that has to be described by the categories of the I-thou (Thou) relationship: *Gegenwart* (presence), *Schicksal* (destiny), freedom, being.

What Buber has to say about God is no theology; it is not an account of God, of his being, his acts, his attributes, his omnipotence, his wisdom, and so forth. The fact is that theology, like philosophy, is a human stance in which the reality—God or being —is made into an object of thought, into a thing. But God cannot be a "thing", an It, which thought represents to itself in order to know it. The sole definition of God, therefore, is this: that he is "the eternal Thou"—that is, he is not to be defined, not to be described, and can be "known" only by means of consecrated obedience and the wager of faith. ["God is] the *Thou* that by its nature cannot become *It*" (*I and Thou*, p. 75; *Werke* I:128). God is the one upon whom we men may call, but even when he makes himself known, he is the "unknown" God.

We thus have life with God—but not theology; we have the eternal Thou, not a "God thing".[1] The question as to whether

[1] Buber writes about the *Gott-Ding* on several occasions—for instance, in *Ich und Du* (*Werke* I:154). By *Gott-Ding* he means God as an object of belief, of cogitation, of cult. This God, whom we "have" because he in fact belongs in the It-world, is not the real, not the living God, not the God who summons us and sends us out into the world. God IS only as the eternal Thou.

theology may be something more than the attempt, located in the I-It situation, to give a detached account of the God-thing which man has or thinks he has is one that Buber does not raise, and we shall not try to answer it here. At all events it is clear enough by now that neither in *Ich und Du* nor in the later writings—for example, in *Gottesfinsternis* (*The Darkness of God*) (1952)— should we look to Buber for a theology. In the nature of things, therefore—and in this he does no more than maintain an ancient Jewish tradition—he is not too concerned about this or that con-tradistinction in theology. Such things are just a posterior out-come or reflection of an encounter with the eternal Thou, or— under another aspect—the frozen icons and traditions of a faith no longer *living*.

Thus Buber contrives to say things that will cause a theologian to tremble. In a context, for instance, in which two people are discussing religious divisions and factions and their effects—per-secutions, the Inquisition, wars, and so forth—one of them says that they should not speak of God here; in his opinion the word is excessively misused. The other says: "Of course. They draw caricatures and write 'God' underneath; they do away with each other, claiming that they act 'in God's name.' But when all delusion, all deceit, is shattered, when in the dark they come to stand alone in his presence and no longer say 'He', but all sigh only 'Thou', cry only 'Thou'—if then in so doing they say 'God', is it not in that case the real God whom they all invoke, the one *living* God. . . . Is it not he who hears them, who answers them?" (*Werke* I:509).

That is clever logic, but is it also true? Was it all nothing but caricature? Did it all amount to delusion and deceit? Is it not at least conceivable—not to say likely—that in one of the darkest periods of European history, in the 16th and 17th centuries, genu-ine issues were at stake? Is it possible, for instance, that the future of Europe was in the balance, as well as the future of European man who had to hold the caricatures at bay in order to live by God? Is it not conceivable that all this had to do with God himself, with his will and his name, and that the point at issue was the reality of the living God, even in all the theological disputa-tions being carried on at that time? Undoubtedly, *hominum confusione et Dei providentia Helvetia regitur*, and folly and

delusion enter the picture far too often. It was a dubious story—
and sometimes not just dubious but downright terrible. And yet
some decision must be made, when God and man—always the
two together—are the stakes involved. "If Yahweh is God, follow him; and if Baal, follow him" (1 Kgs. 18, 21). Even though it
may be true that in the end all our discourse about God is so
much misleading talk, and that we shall never get further than
this recurrent *Irr-rede* (mistaken talk) (*I and Thou*, p. 75;
Werke I:128), it is possible that one sort of mistaken talk can be
of service to the truth—the truth, that is, of a real living together
of God and men—which the other sort contradicts. In that case it
is not permitted to man to retreat into the aloof tolerance which
descries nothing but *Irr-rede* here, there and everywhere. There
are knots to be severed, for instance, by sound reasoning and by
saying as well as possible what there is to be said. That is part and
parcel of the I-It framework, to be sure; yet all kinds of things
are said about God within that framework which might serve to
ensure that "Thou" is not spoken to Baal.

Buber was himself well aware that there are roads to "salvation" which have to be rejected. That applies, for example, to the
Indian religions, particularly Buddhism, and it also applies to
mysticism. One of the Upanishads tells how Indra comes before
Pradjapati, the creator spirit, to learn from him how the self is to
be found and known. After waiting for a thousand years he
receives the reply: "When someone is lying in a dreamless sleep,
that is the self, the immortal, the permanent, the all-being." Indra
departs, but returns with the thought that a man in such a state
no longer knows concerning himself: "That is I" nor even:
"Those are the others." And Pradjapati confirms that it is so.

The self that distinguishes here from there, itself from the
others, must be annihilated. The oneness of being must be experienced—or rather, *not* experienced, for in experience there is still
a distance between the one who experiences and what is experienced. A state of being which is no longer experience, which is
not even dreaming, a state of being which is nothing, Nirvana—
that is the true self. The way of salvation indicated here leads—to
speak in Martin Buber's language—to the extinction of the
I-Thou relation; it means the end of a human mode of existence.
"His innermost decision seems to rest on the extinction of the

ability to say *Thou*," Buber says of the Buddha (*I and Thou*, p.
92; *Werke* I:140). God, the gods and men—all are destined to be
enfolded within the great silence of Nirvana.

But just how essential the "Thou" is for man, and how it asserts
its validity—this Thou which is there prior to every encounter
(cf. *I and Thou*, p. 80; *Werke* I:132)—is demonstrated by the
later history of Buddhism. In Mahayana Buddhism the eternal
Thou is once more invoked—by the name of Buddha! Likewise,
in mysticism there is the absorption of the I in the eternal Thou,
in virtue of which I and Thou both recede into the union, the
unio mystica, that enfolds them. "Ein und ein vereinet," as Master
Eckhardt so finely expresses it. To be assured that the relation
between God and man is to be seen as an I-thou (Thou) relationship surely involves rejecting mysticism—that mysticism, at any
rate, in which "Thou" ceases to be spoken (*I and Thou*, p. 84;
Werke I:134). But does not Christ say in St. John's gospel: "I
and the Father are one" (Jn. 10, 30)? Indeed he does, but that is
to be interpreted not in a mystical sense but in terms of the world
of the Old Testament. "The Father and the Son, like in being
(*wesensgleich*)—we may even say God and Man, like in being—
are the indissolubly real pair, the two bearers of the primal relation which from God to man is termed mission and command,
from man to God is termed looking and hearing, and between
both is termed knowledge and love. In this relation the Son,
though the Father dwells and works in him, bows down before
the 'greater' and prays to him" (*I and Thou*, p. 85; *Werke*
I:135). It is questionable whether the christology of the Johan-
nine gospel is properly reflected here, and whether the transition
from the Father and the Son to God and man can be made in this
way; however, this part of *Ich und Du* is material in this respect,
because Buber shows that for John any idea that the Father and
the Son "are made one" is out of the question and that his gospel is
speaking of something other than mystical union.

In the meantime the question as to the truth of mysticism
cannot be pushed aside by simply pointing to the Gospel, for we
have in the mystics a crowd of witnesses to the fact that indeed
"ein und ein vereinet". May we question their veracity? No.

But within the setting of the I-Thou relation, the event of
which the mystics speak is a marginal event. They are raised in

ecstasy up to, and beyond, the borders of that "over against" which constitutes the essential human situation. It is indeed possible, therefore, for it to happen, but that is *randhaft* (on the brink of being) (*I and Thou*, pp. 85-86; *Werke* I:137).

Where both these ways to salvation are principally at fault is not in anything they say about the relation between God and man, but in their repudiation of the world, of this earthly state of things in which we have to live. The Buddhist monk knows that this world is Maya, an illusory world which lures men and holds them in thrall, which enmeshes them in suffering and alienates them from the true self. The wise man will forsake this world. As against this Buber says (and what he says has tremendous consequences): "There is no illusory world; there is only the world" (*I and Thou*, p. 77; *Werke* I:129). Man is not to forsake this world. And as far as the mystic is concerned, in the world of Judaism and of Christianity he certainly cannot go as far as the Buddhist monk, for he knows with certainty that the world is God's creation, a creation which God has himself willed, and has seen that it is good. Yet he too must turn away from the world to seek the way to God. Mysticism begins in ascesis, in asceticism.

In both Buddhism and mysticism, therefore, man has to choose between the world, which changes and passes away, and God or being, the self, the imperishable, the "highest and eternal good".

Now Buber opposes this with all the strength at his command. The world is not something to be "seen through" and abandoned; it must be known and hallowed. Man is not called out of the world; he is sent into it. "I know nothing of a 'world' and a 'life in the world' that might separate a man from God. What is thus described is actually life which experiences and uses an alienated world of *It*. He who truly goes out to meet the world goes out also to God. Concentration (*Sammlung*) and outgoing are necessary, both in truth, at once the one and the other, which is the One" (*I and Thou*, p. 95; *Werke* I:142). We take note of the fact that in order to find God and to receive his presence (*Gegenwart*) man has indeed to forsake a world—namely, the world of having and experiencing and using, the world in which God is not. But to forsake that It-world is not to turn away from the world. On the contrary, it is the one thing necessary if we are to be *wholly* in the world and are to find God and people in it. "True love for God begins with love for people" (*Werke* I:305).

Stated in another way, relationship to the eternal Thou begins in our earthly relationships, in humble devotion and service to men; it begins with a "being-in-the-world", a being that refuses to be engrossed in having and using. If Kierkegaard had had *faith*, he would have remained with Regine. That is what Jesus meant by the great commandment (Mt. 22: 37-40): "By binding the two together into one—namely, love for God and love for man—Jesus brings out the Old Testament truth that God and man are not rivals. The exclusive (*ausschliessliche*) love of God is, *because he is God*, a comprehensive (*einschliessliche*) love" (*Werke* I:229).

In this passage from his study of Kierkegaard, Buber points to the Bible, to the Old and New Testaments. Elsewhere he directs us to Chassidism, where this *einschliessliche*, this world-embracing love, is recognized and lived out—in all respects, according to Buber, although Gershom Scholem contradicts him on this score. In the Preface to the short book in which Buber has summarized the teachings of Rabbi Israel ben Eliezer, the Baal Shem Tov—a book which appeared in 1927, soon after *Ich und Du*—he gives an account of Chassidic "mysticism" which bears a different stamp from, for example, that of Master Eckhardt. It is a "realist" mysticism, "a mysticism which does not look upon the world as an illusion from which man must turn away in order to attain to true being, but as the reality between God and man . . . as the object of the creative message addressed to man, and as the object of his service in which he makes his response, as the reality destined to be redeemed by the meeting of God's actions with those of men" (*Werke* III:49). The *chassiduth* of this Polish Jew, which implicates the world in the relation of God and man, may best be defined, according to Buber, as cherishing the world in God. We may leave aside the question whether the Baal Shem Tov was in fact responsible for teaching this *chassiduth*. At all events for Buber such a "realist" mysticism is the heart of all true piety.

There is one observation in this passage over which we must pause for a moment. The concern of this mysticism is with the redemption of the world: not man's redemption from the world, or his deliverance from it, but that redemption wherein the world, as God's creation, is itself redeemed. It has to do with the *Yichud*—that process by which God and man and world are

made one together, and all separation and alienation, all opposi-
tions and counterdistinctions, are brought to an end, but without
the disappearance of the "over against", of the confrontation
between God and man. Of this redemption Buber says that it is
not the work of God and it is not the work of men; it is the work
of God and men together. Redemption is possible only "through
the encounter between the actions of God and those of men".
Dieu a besoin des hommes: God has need of men. It is the measure of man's greatness that it is partly through his humble obedience to God's will that redemption is accomplished, just as it is
a measure of God's greatness that he has put his work into the
hands of men. A step further, and we are with Rilke and with the
questions in the *Stundenbuch:*

> *Was wirst du tun, Gott, wenn ich sterbe?*
> *Ich bin dein Krug (wenn ich zerscherbe?)*
> *Ich bin dein Trank (wenn ich verderbe?)*
> *Bin dein Gewand und dein Gewerbe,*
> *Mit mir verlierst du deinen Sinn.*

> What wilt thou do, God, should I die?
> I am thy vessel (should I be shattered)?
> I am thy drink (should I be spoilt?)
> I am thy clothing and thy calling;
> With me, thine import too is lost.

But this is a step which Buber does not take. Admittedly, he is
convinced that it is up to me; it comes down in the end to my
decision to obey God's will or to resist it, to my prayer and my
sacrifice. "You know always in your heart that you need God
more than everything, but do you not also know that God needs
you, that in the fullness of his eternity he needs you? How would
man be, how would you be, if God did not need him, did not
need you? You need God in order to be—and God needs you.
. . . There is divine meaning in the life of the world, of man, of
human persons, of you and of me" (*I and Thou*, p. 82; *Werke*
I:133). A little further on Buber writes about the petition in the
Lord's Prayer "Thy will be done" and about the man who commits his will to God: " 'Thy will be done,' he says, and says no
more; but truth adds for him: 'through me whom Thou need-
est' " (*I and Thou*, p. 83; *Werke* I:133).

Is it indeed the truth that adds this clause to the other? Is that what the Lord's Prayer and the New Testament are tacitly saying to us? Is it true, as Buber said in an address, delivered in 1916, on "Der Geist des Judentums" ("The Genius of Judaism"), that God is actualized by man, and that this is the religious *Akt* (deed)? Is it true, as he says in the same address, that we should not believe in God but should actualize him, hew him out of the stone of this world in which his countenance invisibly resides? Is it true, as Buber says a little later on in *Ich und Du*, that there is a becoming, not of the God that is coming to be but of the God that is (*I and Thou*, p. 82; *Werke* I:133)? And if it is true, are we not very close, after all, to Rilke and his notes—in his diaries and his letters to Ellen Key—to the effect that we have to build God and that he comes to be in us and through us, as does a medieval cathedral, through the hands of men? There *is* a difference, for Rilke knows only of the God who is becoming, whereas with Buber it is the God that *is* who is becoming. For Rilke there can be no question of dialogue, whereas for Buber God is the eternal Thou. And yet, in this "realist" mysticism more is entrusted to man than he is capable of accomplishing. "Thy will be done" by me—that has to be said, but it must also be done in spite of me and in spite of my recalcitrance and my confusion.

Or is it something different again that is at issue: not the "actualizing" of God, but his presence and his "palpability"? While remaining true to his earlier conception, Buber moves in his later writings—in *Gottesfinsternis*, for instance—in that direction. In them the relationship of God and man is again one of faith. In them the relationship of God to men no longer contains any element of "wanting in order to use" (*brauchen*), but rather—and this is something very different—an element of "needing" (*bedürfen*), and the *bedürfen* is a situation which God has himself willed. In these later writings too, man's part in the course of God's dealings with the world is changed. Man does not actualize God; he is empowered only to contribute to the *Offenbarkeit* (openness) and hiddenness of God (*Werke* I:559). The structure of the "realist" mysticism is still there, but some fundamental modifications have been introduced, and these make the thinking more realistic in character.

If we ask where God is to be found, the answer therefore is: in the world. If we ask how God is to be found, it must first be said that there is no *one* way to God and that it is thus impossible to say what way a man should take. There is no trace of "method-ism" in what Buber writes. Even so, something may be said about the "turning round", the *teshuwah*, which is a precondition for meeting with God. A man must be ready to abandon the world established by the primary word, I-It. He must be prepared to abandon that stance of self-preservation which tied him down to the world—but only so that he could "have" and could protect himself—and which separated him in the world from reality. He must have the courage to enter into the solitude that fits a man to set foot in the holy of holies. He must surrender his own will, so as to be able to conform himself to the will of God. The list is endless, but there is no rule, no prescription to say clearly what must be done; there are only words, pointing to what cannot be said. As to whether God will be found at the end of it all, that is not for us to decide. That is his doing, his revelation.

Revelation

To get a clear idea of what Buber means by "revelation" we must take a careful look at a part of *Ich und Du*. What is revela-tion? Buber says: "It is the phenomenon that a man does not pass from the moment of the supreme meeting the same being as he entered into it. The moment of meeting is not an 'experience' (*Erlebnis*). . . .[2] Rather, in that moment something happens to

---

[2] The word *Erlebnis* is left in here because in the language of psy-chology it has acquired a very special significance. Buber is here setting himself against psychology and against a psychological interpretation—that is, against a whittling away of the character of revelation as event. It is in fact no psychic occurrence, but something which happens between God and man. In itself there is nothing against a psychological appraisal of what takes place in man apropos of this event between God and man—but that is not the way to get through to the real nature of the event itself. Faith is not a sensation, a "feeling" (*Werke* I:505) any more than love is a "feeling" (*Werke* I:87). It is a happening. "One has feelings; love, however, takes place" (*Werke* I:87). Psychology does not come to grips with the reality of faith or of love, but only with the psychical *Erlebnis*, which is given along with the faith or with the love. This demarcation of happen-ing and *Erlebnis*, of reality and inwardness, is of importance when one is considering the implications of the *Gottesfinsternis*.

the man. At times it is like a light breath, at times like a wrestling
bout, but always it *happens*. . . .[3] The reality is that we receive
what we did not hitherto have, and receive it in such a way that
we know it has been given to us. In the language of the Bible,
'Those who wait upon the Lord shall renew their strength' (Is.
40, 31). . . . Man receives, and he receives not a specific content
but a Presence (*Gegenwart*),[4] a Presence as power. This Presence and this power include three things, undivided, yet in such a
way that we may consider them separately. First, there is the
whole fullness of real mutual action, of being raised and bound
up in relation: the man can give no account at all of how the
binding in relation is brought about, nor does it in any way
lighten his life—it makes life heavier, but heavy with meaning.
Second, there is the inexpressible confirmation of meaning. Meaning is assured. Nothing can any longer be meaningless. The question about the meaning of life is no longer there. But were it
there, it would not have to be answered. You do not know how
to exhibit and define the meaning of life, you have no formula or
picture for it, and yet it has more certitude for you than the
perceptions of your senses. What does the revealed and concealed
meaning propose to us, desire from us? It does not wish to be
explained (nor are we able to do that) but only to be done by us.
Third, this meaning is not that of 'another life', but that of this
life of ours, not one of a world 'out there' but that of this world
of ours, and it desires its confirmation in this life and in relation
with this world.[5] This meaning can be received, but not experi-

[3] Buber is here probably thinking of Elijah (I Kgs. 19, 12) or of the
vision in Job 4, 12ff., and in the last instance, probably, of Jacob's wrestling
with the angel (Gen. 32, 22-32).

[4] This translation of *Gegenwart* as "Presence" is of course a feasible one;
the German word has been left standing in the text, however, because
Gegenwart gives point to the fact that God and man are *two*, as the word
"Presence" does not, and for Buber a great deal depends on the fact that
God and man are not identical, that God really is the Other, and not "the
ground of my ground" (Joan Luyken).

[5] *Bewährt*, rendered here by "confirmed" ("confirmation") is scarcely
translatable. The significance that the word possesses for Buber is evident
from the fact that in his translation of the Old Testament the Hebrew
tsaddik is rendered as *der Bewährte*. Thus Psalm 1, 6, for example, runs:
ER kennt den Weg der Bewährten (HE knows the way of the tried, the
proven ones), while in Psalm 11, 3 we read: *Der Bewährte—was kann er
wirken?* (The tried, the proven one—what may he do?) Now this passage

enced; it cannot be experienced[6] but it can be done, and this is its purpose with us. The assurance I have of it does not wish to be sealed within me, but it wishes to be borne by me into the world. But just as the meaning itself does not permit itself to be transmitted and made into knowledge generally current and admissible, so confirmation of it cannot be transmitted as a valid 'ought';[7] it is not prescribed, it is not specified on any tablet, to be raised above all men's heads. . . . That before which, in which, out of which, and into which we live, even the mystery, has remained what it was. It has become present to us and in its presentness has proclaimed itself to us as salvation; we have 'known' it, but we acquire no knowledge from it which might lessen or moderate its mysteriousness. We have come near to God, but not nearer to unveiling being or solving its riddle. . . . We cannot approach others with what we have received and say: 'You must know this; you must do this.' We can only seek to confirm its truth. And this, too, is no 'ought', but 'we can', 'we *must*' " (*I and Thou*, pp. 109-11; *Werke* I:152-154).

A few comments on this passage, which presents us with the whole essence of Buber's thought, may help to bring somewhat closer to us what he has in view.

Buber's thinking on the subject of revelation is clearly orientated upon the Old Testament. Yet the passage is in no way an

---

in *Ich und Du* was written before Buber, together with Franz Rosenzweig, had started on the translation of the Old Testament, but it is not impossible (it is even likely) that the Chassidic *tsaddik* was already present to Buber's mind here. This individual then—"the righteous one" is what it says in the (Dutch) New Translation—is not marked by his fidelity to the law in the ordinary sense, but by the direct relationship to God which enables him to enact and to substantiate (confirm) in this life and in this world the meaning which "it" has. Besides the translation given here, the rendering "are loyal to . . ." is deserving of consideration.

[6] Because experience is in fact one of the categories of the world that is *gegründet* (established) by the primary word I-It. The meaning that requires something to be *done* and is given in the doing itself is no It that we can reflect upon and express in words.

[7] "Thou shalt . . .": The German here is *sollen* ("to be obliged", "to be in duty bound . . ."); but the word is more reminiscent of Kant and his ethics than of the law, graven in stone, which Buber evidently has in mind. True religion is not "legalistic"; it is not a relationship to a law given us by God, but is a relationship to God himself: the relationship, that is, of *tsedākāh*, fidelity to the meaning which we are given to know in the doing of it.

account of what took place between Yahweh and Israel or her Chassidim. It is a description of the primary phenomenon (*Urphä-nomen*) of revelation; in other words, every real revelation of God to us men has this structure, and if something occurs which does not have this structure, it is not—whatever else it may be—a real revelation of God.

Revelation is not a communicating of "truths" about God, man and the world which can be consolidated into a system of dogma, a system that is the work of men, naturally, but nevertheless has its source in God. This notion of revelation—and it is to be found in many Churches—is an erroneous one, if only because it locates revelation wholly within the I-It framework, the very thing that we must abandon if we are to be able to find God.

It simply cannot be said that God reveals himself, for this would imply that God must be his own *Gegenstand*, his own object. "God does not create himself; he does not redeem himself; when he 'reveals himself', it is not himself that he reveals. Even his revelation does not have him as its object" (*Werke* I:230). This means, among other things, that revelation does not refer man to God but to the world and to the work that is to be done in it. "Meeting with God does not come to man in order that he may concern himself with God, but in order that he may confirm (*bewährt*) that there is meaning in the world" (*I and Thou*, p. 115; *Werke* I:157). Man, however, does what he should not do. "*Er will sich statt mit der Welt mit Gott befassen*" ("He wishes to concern himself with God instead of with the world") (*I and Thou*, p. 115; *Werke* I:157) and so is untrue to his proper task. Cult usurps the place that should belong to the business of "realizing" and hallowing the world.

Of this happening and of what it has effected in their lives—for I become a different person from the one I was before—men are able to speak. But when they talk about the inexpressible—which is not "some thing"—this already implies a changed situation. The I-Thou relation is abandoned; a man will speak of "it" and of "him", but cannot say what has taken place. The situation is one of "having no word for it, and no image". Of revelation only a "stumbling account" (*stammelnde Kunde: Werke* I:512) is possible. What men say is so much stumbling human speech, and not the Word of God. For Buber, to equate the scriptures with the

Word of God is an impossibility. Of course, the stumbling speech of men may well lead to a new encounter and to a new occurrence of revelation, and that is why Buber bestowed so much care on the rendering of the Old Testament.

If revelation is event—the occurring of a Presence (*Gegenwart*)—still it does not follow that the man who is involved in this event "has" God from then on. When Moses is sent to Egypt ("*Führe mein Volk, die Söhne Jissraels, aus Aegypten*"—"Lead my people, the sons of Israel, out of Egypt": Ex. 3, 10), he wants to know above all else the name of the One who is sending him. In other words, regardless of anything else, he wants to be sure of God—and that is not possible:

> *Ich werde dasein, als der ich dasein werde ...*
> *So sollst du zu den Söhnen Jissraels sprechen:*
> *ICH BIN DA strickt mich zu euch* (Ex. 3, 14).

> I will be that I will be. ...
> Thus shalt thou say to the sons of Israel:
> I AM (THERE) sends me to you (Ex. 3, 14).

Yet the God who conceals his name from Moses is the God who is present, who is at hand. He withdraws into an awful presence which makes life *sinnschwer* (charged with meaning) —and that is all. The faith required of Moses is not a kind of "having" but an act of trusting, of confiding. In whom? That cannot be said; it is in the nameless "I am (there)".

Every image of God, every concept of God, therefore, is a human contrivance intended to pin God down and to end the situation in which men "have no word for him and no image". People want to see God and to have him near them: a figure in the temple, an icon in the living room, a block of wood to pray to, a map—however rough it may be—of his ways. That is why the Law permits *no* images. An image is, as a matter of fact, *Festlegung auf eine Offenbarkeit* (*Werke* I:748)—i.e., an attempt to preserve some "disclosure-situation" in a fixed and settled form. Buber knows very well that images do not just happen, but have their source in real encounters, and he also knows that they may be highly compatible with an authentic relationship to God as the eternal Thou. He goes further still in recognizing that certain symbols are indispensable—for instance, the symbol of God as a Person (*Werke* I:169) who can be invoked and who answers. But in all images and symbols God remains the hidden One. No image can survive in the crucible of revelation. As Franz Rosenzweig says: "*Alle Offenbarung beginnt mit einem grossen Nein*" ("Every revelation begins with a mighty 'No' ").

The sort of happenings described in this part of *Ich und Du* does not make life easier. It changes the man overtaken by it, and it changes the order of his life. Encounter with God assuredly makes life a thing charged with meaning (*sinnschwer*), but it first of all upsets the meaning that I had given it. T. S. Eliot's magi, after their journey to Bethlehem, knew that they were witnesses to a death—namely, to their own death.[8] In this passage that is not clearly evident. It becomes so, however, when in *Gottesfinsternis* Buber cites with approval Whitehead's view that religion is a movement from God the void to God the enemy, and then to God the companion. Where at first there was a void, God enters into life as an enemy, and the enemy turns out to be the companion. Buber meant by this that in our living and in our thinking about God we cannot start with love. The real God is "*zunächst furchtbar und unverständlich*" ("in the first place dreadful and incomprehensible") (*Werke* I:530).

This event is one that affords no view or prospect of another and a better world, of a life after death, of heaven. Along with Karl Marx and Friedrich Nietzsche and the whole of existentialism Buber opposes the dualistic division of the world into "here" and "there", this world and another "set in the clouds" (Karl Marx); he opposes all Platonism (even in its Christian manifestation) that alienates man from the earth and from history. Meaning demands to be confirmed or "tested" (*bewährt*) in this life and in this world. The *tsaddik* is, as Nietzsche would say, loyal to the earth, and if in the encounter a future is disclosed, then that is this earth's future—the *yichud*, the prospect of unifying what is chaotic and unintegrated. Because in his love God is comprehensive (*einschliesslich*), because he embraces in his love the whole

---

[8] T. S. Eliot, "The Journey of the Magi," in *Collected Poems 1909-1935* (London,[17] 1959), p. 108:

    ". . . this Birth was
Hard and bitter agony for us, like Death, our death."

of reality, for that very reason man is sent into the world. The Chassidim's activist mysticism is not an arbitrary device on man's part, but springs from the encounter, in consequence of which a man becomes a different being from what he was before.

Finally, the author of *Ich und Du* was always engaged with problems of nurture and education. This section shows that he did not find it an easy matter. He has "nothing to say". He has no theory, no doctrine which he can expound, so that we can take his word for it. He cannot say who God is or what he wants of us. He can only speak incoherently of what he has been given to know—and what he says is not the truth. In fact, the truth cannot be said; it can only be *performed*. He comes pretty near to St. Augustine's "Ama Deum et fac quod vis" ("Hold God dear, and then do what you wish—nay, what you must do"). He has no defense against the power of the ideologies that can drown his voice because their aims and purposes are so clear. What he says may be shrugged off and thrust aside as being neither here nor there; there is nothing to it. Meanwhile man is overwhelmed by Heidegger's structure (*Gestell*) and by Buber's It-world, and the *Gottesfinsternis*, the darkness of God, descends upon the earth.

Gottesfinsternis (*The Eclipse of God*)

Implicit in everything that Buber says about God and men is one major question: Is he talking about a Reality which can indeed encounter man, or is he one of the last to concern himself with a great illusion—an illusion which people have now seen through? Is there indeed a God, or must we envisage things, in whatever fashion we may elect to do so, without God?

In the early part of the 19th century Hölderlin spoke of the absence of God:

Aber weh! es wandelt in Nacht, es wohnt, wie im Orkus
ohne Göttliches, unser Geschlecht ...

Alas and alas! It walks in night, it dwells as it were in Orcus,
our generation, without the Divine.

Here already we have the absence of the Divine (*Göttlich*)

associated with the onset of night—a connection made again by Nietzsche, by Heidegger and in Buber's *Gottesfinsternis*.

At the close of the 19th century, in the year 1882, Nietzsche in *Die fröhliche Wissenschaft* (*The Joyful Wisdom*) described the man who during the afternoon walks around the marketplace with a lantern in his hand looking for God: the God who no longer is, who is dead; and though it is only afternoon, the lanterns have to be lit, because it grows dark, and even darker still, upon the earth. A few years later Zoroaster became the interpreter of a new gospel which had become necessary after the death of the God who was *Menschen-Werk und -Wahnsinn* ("the fabrication of men, and their lunacy").[9] What Nietzsche said about the death of God has in our time been taken up by Martin Heidegger[10] and Jean-Paul Sartres,[11] and though the third major exponent of existentialism, Karl Jaspers, says a good deal about *Transzendenz*, for him too the God whose demise was proclaimed by Nietzsche—the eternal Thou—would seem to be dead.[12]

In the meantime Feuerbach had already written *Das Wesen der Religion* (*The Essence of Religion*) in which he had expounded the view that theology is in fact anthropology. Karl Marx had also suggested to his contemporaries that they must part company with the *phantastiche Verwirklichung* of man (i.e., his fanciful mode of realization), which is religion, and must live from then on without opium. Auguste Comte had made it clear that the theological and metaphysical stage of history is behind us and that we have at last reached the point where it is possible to see within the process how things *really* cohere. In the 20th century Henri Bergson joined the ranks of Marx, Nietzsche and the rest. He saw in the gods a creation of the human *fonction fabulatrice*. Finally Sigmund Freud entitled his book on religion *Die Zukunft*

[9] Fr. Nietzsche, *Die fröhliche Wissenschaft*, Fragment 125 (*Werke* II: 126-28); *Also sprach Zarathustra* (*Werke* II:297).

[10] M. Heidegger, "Nietzsches Wort: Gott ist tot," in *Holzwege* (Frankfurt a.M., 1950), pp. 193-247; "Wer ist Nietzsches Zarathustra?" in *Vortraege und Aufsaetze* (Pfullingen, 1954), pp. 101-26. On Heidegger and the theme of the death of God, cf. M. Buber, *Werke* I:555-61.

[11] J-P. Sartre, "Un nouveau mystique," in *Situations* I (Paris, 1947), especially p. 153; *L'être et le néant* (Paris, 1943), pp. 286f. On Sartre and the "death of God" motif, cf. M. Buber, *Werke* I:550-55.

[12] Cf. Buber's critique of Jaspers in *Werke* I:301-04.

einer Illusion (*The Future of an Illusion*), stating that religious ideas are illusions in which the most ancient and powerful yearnings of mankind find their fulfillment.[13]

Is it possible to maintain that when it comes to the relationship of man to "God" we are dealing with anything real? That is the question posed in *Gottesfinsternis*.[14] There is no proving anything, of course. The proofs of God's existence belong to an age that lies far behind us, even if Thomistic philosophy still contends that the proofs advanced in St. Thomas' *Summa Theologica* are valid ones. Therefore, Buber offers no proof of anything. Here again he is the defenseless witness to Reality against the *Irrealisierung Gottes* (*Werke* 1:515)—the attenuation of God's reality—which he sees as already having started before Feuerbach in Kant and Hegel. As an old man, Kant did indeed say (in his posthumous annotations to be found in Volume XXI/XXII of the edition of his works prepared by the Prussian Academy of Sciences, which implement the line of argument in his Critiques: "*Gott ist nicht ein Wesen ausser mir, sondern bloss ein Gedanke in mir*" ("God is not a Being outside of me, but only an idea within me") (*Werke* I:541). The relationship to God then ceases to be a real relationship: "God" is a relation in which man relates himself to himself; he is "*bloss ein moralisches Verhältnis in mir*" ("purely a moral relationship in me"). This is a road which, if pursued, leads eventually to the psychologizing of religion and ultimately to the "religious projection" thesis, as championed in The Netherlands by Vestdijk and Sierksma[15]—the latter doing so far more convincingly and with stronger arguments than the former.

[13] Cf. in connection with the foregoing paragraph Dr. H. de Vos, *Inleiding tot de wijsbegeerte van den godsdienst* (Assen, 1937), pp. 144-55.

[14] The word is formed by analogy with *Sonnenfinsternis* (solar eclipse), and its meaning is best conveyed, therefore, as the "eclipse (i.e., obfuscation) of God". In this book Buber brings together several essays which had in part already appeared earlier. The piece entitled *Religion und modernes Denken* had appeared, for example, in Feb., 1952, in *Merkur* VI:2. These papers are thematically interrelated, but there is no overall systematic development of the ideas. The subtitle, aptly enough, refers to *Betrachtungen* (reflections).

[15] S. Vestdijk, *De toekomst der religie* (Arnhem,[2] 1952). Fokke Sierksma, *Tussen twee vuren* (Amsterdam, 1952). *Idem*, "De religieuze projectie," in *Algemeen Nederlands Tijdschrift voor wijsbegeerte en psychologie* (Jaargang 50:186-94).

What is of greatest interest in *Gottesfinsternis* is not the argument deployed against Jean-Paul Sartre (*Werke* I:550-555) and
Martin Heidegger (*Werke* I:555-561) but the attack on the work
of "the leading psychologist of our day", C. G. Jung (*Werke*
I:561-574). Of course, Buber is not opposed to a psychological
approach to religion as a phenomenon, but only to a psychology
that oversteps the mark and ventures to make pronouncements of
a metaphysical and "theological" variety. In Jung's work such
does happen. In *Psychologische Typen*, for example, he talks
about a reciprocal relation between man and God, and this makes
it look as if he has in view an I-Thou relationship. But when
Jung expatiates further on this, man becomes "a psychic function of God" and God becomes "a psychic function of man", or
even "a function of the unconscious"; Jung also goes on to say
that there is an opposition between this psychological conception
of God and the orthodox one, according to which God *für sich
existiert* (exists by himself). Thus God is a function of the unconscious, engendering images which man projects outside himself and to which he attributes an independent existence (*für
sich*) until he sees the game for what it is and retracts the images
into himself again. What that in fact implies is the replacement of
the fundamental relation to the Other by a self-contained psychic
condition, an *Irrealisierung Gottes*, and it also involves overstep-
ping the bounds between psychology and metaphysics. "To put
it crudely: for all that this psychology assures us that it is no
Weltanschauung but science, it will not be satisfied with the role
of an interpreter of religion; it proclaims the new religion—the
only one that can still be *true*—the religion of 'psychic im-
manence'" (*Werke* I:567).

Buber does not deny, of course, that in the thesis of religious
projection there is a large element of truth. All pronouncements
about God are human pronouncements, and all images are a
human product. But faith's intention is focused via the images or
in the images upon the Unenvisaged, the imageless One, who IS.
These words "who IS", which are not open to proof but arise out
of an elementary experience,[16] denote the boundary between

[16] In Buber's later writings "experience" is no longer a category of the
I-It relation. If according to *Ich und Du* experience is matched with *Du-
Ferne* (Werke I:83; cf. *I and Thou*, p. 9: "In the act of experience *Thou*

faith and the "modern consciousness": "Most certainly, the modern consciousness . . . has an aversion to faith.[17] But it will not do to state the consequences of that aversion in terms which are presented as if they were strictly psychological pronouncements. Neither psychology nor any other science is competent to inquire into the truth-value of faith in God" (*Werke* I: 602).

The argument in *Gottesfinsternis* is not simply concerned, in any event, with certain changes in human consciousness—changes which are foreshadowed in Kant and from which C. G. Jung has drawn the ultimate consequences in what purport to be his psychological utterances but are in fact metaphysical ones. An eclipse of the sun occurs whenever the moon passes between the sun and the earth; for a brief period the earth is something "not there" for the sun, and the sun is invisible to the earth. It is not only that something has happened with man; something has occurred "between" God and men. "Something has come between." What has come between? What is this *Dazwischentretende* (intervening) thing (*Werke* I: 597)? It is man himself— that is, the man of the I-It relationship, who has made himself master of the earth and "has driven the man of the I-Thou relationship into the catacombs" (*Werke* I: 599). Therefore, the fact that God is obscured, is eclipsed, is not the same thing as the hiddenness or even the "absence" of God, although we must not lose sight altogether here of the motif of the God who hides himself (Is. 45, 15; cf. *Werke* I: 551). God is not hidden or "absent", but man finds himself blocking the way to God, and God blocking the way to men. It is man himself who is *dazwischengetreten*, who has come in between.

"In our time the I-It relation . . . has taken over control, almost unchallenged. The I of this relation—an I that has everything, makes everything, is never at a loss for anything, is unable to say

is far away"), in *Gottesfinsternis* Buber talks about the "experience" of faith and that a man can look up to God—"There is no other authority for this save that of faith; it is not to be demonstrated; it is only to be experienced. Man *has* experienced it" (*Werke* I: 597). What the reason is for this striking modification in Buber's use of language we cannot say. He has not offered any explanation himself.

[17] Buber is referring here to a passage in C. G. Jung, *Seelenprobleme der Gegenwart* (*Problems of the Psyche at the Present Time*), where Jung says: The modern consciousness recoils from faith and thus also from the religions based upon it" (cf. *Werke* I: 566).

'thou' or have any real meeting with another—is lord and master of this hour. Not unnaturally, this I, grown thus almighty and encompassed by that total It, cannot recognize God. It 'gets in between' and blocks all passage to the heavenly light" (*Werke* I:598f.). If it is indeed man himself who has come in between, three consequences flow from that fact. The first is that the *Gottesfinsternis*, the divine darkness, is not some kind of fate to which 20th-century man can do no more than resign himself. The second is that the *teshuwah*, the "turning about", puts an end to the *Gottesfinsternis*. The third is that considered thinking about the obfuscation of the Light of the world may lead us finally to the prospect of a new encounter. "That the divine light is darkened is not to say that it is snuffed out; tomorrow, even, may see the end of what stands in between" (*Werke* I:599)— these are the closing words of the book. The thinking person who has pondered and come to understand their context and coherence has but a single task: to do all that lies within his power to turn the *teshuwah* into reality.

Faith and Faith

It is evident from Martin Buber's writings that throughout his life he was preoccupied with the New Testament and with the Christian faith. Already in *Ich und Du*—that is, in the year 1923 —he is writing about Jesus (*I and Thou*, pp. 66-67; *Werke* I:123) and contrasting him with Napoleon. Even then Buber could have said what many years later he did say: "Jesus is my great brother" (*Werke* I:657). In the history of Israel's faith this "great brother" has meant a very great deal indeed, and he cannot be put into any of the usual categories such as "prophet" and so forth. In view of the history of relations between the Jewish people and Christendom, that is no small thing. Yet Buber stands outside the Christian faith—and that is not the verdict of an inquisitor. The words are his own.

A brochure that was produced in Hamburg in 1926 contains one of Buber's letters in which he expresses the contrast between Judaism and Christianity. He discusses the incident recorded in the New Testament as having taken place in the high north of Galilee, in the region of Caesarea Philippi (Mk. 8, 27-30). Jesus asks his disciples whom or what people see in him, and he gets a variety of answers. He goes on to ask whom or what the disciples themselves see in him, and Peter replies: "Thou art the Christ." Christ, which in the course of the centuries has been worn down by us into a name, is really a title. The Greek word *christos* is actually a translation of the Hebrew *mashiach*. Now in the Jewish world the *mashiach* was the king, but after the fall of Jerusalem in 586 B.C. had brought about the end of the monarchy, the *mashiach*—for reasons not altogether discoverable and through a course of events which we cannot survey in every detail—came over the centuries to be the man who was expected to appear at the end of days in order to complete God's work on earth. That is what Peter implied when he said: "Thou art the Christ." About that declaration on the part of the first disciple Buber has this to say:

"I believe something was said in Caesarea Philippi that was well and truly intended, and yet was not true, and the fact that it has been repeated down the centuries still does not make it true. I believe that God reveals himself not in people, but only *through* them. I believe that the *Mashiach* does not come at a particular moment in history; his coming can only be the end of history. I believe that the world's redemption did not become a fact nineteen centuries ago. We are still living in a world that is not redeemed; we are still looking forward to the redemption—and each of us is called to do his part in the work of redeeming the world.[1] Israel is the community of people which retains this purely messianic expectation, even though the Jews have all too often proved unfaithful to it. That is what Israel always is, what she will be to the end; and because she has her part in the work of accomplishing the end, Israel must sustain her faith in the coming of the kingdom—that is, a faith that the world is not as yet redeemed and that the redemption must come. In our faith, in the faith of Israel, the redemption of the world is one and the same with the finishing of the creation. The man who raises Jesus to so high a place ceases to be one of us, and if he wants to challenge our faith that the redemption lies in the future . . . then we go our separate ways."[2]

That is plain enough. Christian faith—Peter, at any rate—sees Jesus as the Christ, the *Mashiach*, the one who has redeemed the world. Buber, the Jew, repudiates that faith (which raises the question whether he has correctly represented the faith that he rejects). Jesus is not the Christ, and whoever puts him as high as Peter did—according to Mark 8—is no longer one of us.

In the relation of Judaism to Christianity, however, far more is at issue than the question of whether Jesus is the *Mashiach*. The differences go much deeper. It is about these that Buber wrote in

---

[1] Here, then, are the grounds for an activist mysticism: the world will not be redeemed without the collaboration of men and, in the first place, of Israel. The context in which the theme occurs prompts the question whether it is not unreasonable, in Buber's case, to speak of "messianic" mysticism at all. It is indeed not only the work of the *Mashiach*, who is coming at the end, that is "messianic"; also messianic is every activity of men that accords with God's will.

[2] The brochure in which this passage occurs has the title *Höre, Israel*. Cf. in this connection Franz Freiherr von Hammerstein, *Das Messiasproblem bei Martin Buber* (Stuttgart, 1958), p. 49.

a small book *Zwei Glaubensweisen* (*Two Ways of Faith*) which appeared in 1950 (*Werke* I:651-782).

As a preliminary to writing this book he made a conscientious study of the New Testament and the most important literature on the New Testament documents. As his principal guides Buber took Albert Schweitzer, author of the celebrated book *Die Geschichte der Leben-Jesu-Forschung* (*The Jesus of History*), and Rudolf Bultmann, but he also made use of other writings on the New Testament. The fundamental thesis of his book is that "faith" in the Jewish world signifies something different from what it means in Christianity. What matters most is not that they think differently about Jesus in this way or that way, but that the whole relationship of man to God is a different one. On the one hand there is "faith" in the sense of the Jewish *'èmunah*, on the other "faith" in the sense of the Greek *pistis*. Between the two *Glaubensweisen* there is a formal agreement, it is true. Both have to do with my whole being, and thus both are existential and unconditional and incapable of justification by rational arguments, so that I cannot say "why" I believe. Yet for all this formal agreement, they present a mutual contrast. This, when schematized, appears as follows:

'èmunah	*pistis*
trusting	accepting, acknowledging
status	actus
I. community	I. individual
II. individual	II. community
continuity	break with "the old"
Beharren[3] (steadfastness, persistence)	conversion
Jewish	Greek

[3] It is feasible, of course, to translate the word *Beharren* as, for example, "to persevere" or "to stick to one's guns". But for Buber this is one of the essential elements of *'èmunah*, and it seemed preferable, therefore, to let the word stand. To Buber's way of thinking there is no discrepancy between this *Beharren* and the *teshuwah*, in which the condition of "trust", of "reliance", is forever being brought to life. Again, it is a relevant point that even in the Hebrew *'èmunah* there is an element of steadfastness or, better still, of fixedness, immovability. The primary meaning of the verb *'mn*, in fact, is to hold out, to make a firm stand (*Werke* I:670). All this brings us pretty close to the *tsedākāh* which we were talking about earlier. Therefore, *'èmunah* and *tsedākāh* go together, as in the passage from Habakkuk's prophecy which Paul took over and misrepresented in the

In the first case the reference is to trust or confidence—a trust grounded in the dealings of Yahweh with his people. The individual is called to exercise this trust which is no break with the old, but a *Beharren*, a persistent adherence to what is historically given: the covenant of Yahweh with his people. This faith, which is not expressed in formulas having the structure "I believe that . . .", is more a status—something in which, as a part of his race and nation, a man "finds himself" (*Werke* I:654)—than an act, although this status, of course, must continually be turned into a lived reality. That is what occurs in the *teshuwah*—namely, a break with the old, an *Austritt aus der Geschichte* (*Werke* I:780), a "seceding" from historical continuity.

Buber adds—and this is a thing that some critics of *Zwei Glaubensweisen* have overlooked—that elements of the Jewish faith-structure are also present in the Greek, and vice versa, so that it is impossible to give a rounded account of the actual historical situation in terms of a simple contrast (cf., e.g., *Werke* I:654). Buber's account of the two *Glaubensweisen* is meant to typify an ideal. The structures that he discloses are not what we find in the concrete historical situation, but are a kind of divining rod for the historian to employ.

Insofar as the New Testament is concerned, Buber's most important thesis is that the dividing line between the two *Glaubensweisen* runs not between the Old and New Testaments but right across the New Testament itself. The Jewish faith-structure is exemplified in Jesus and is still recognizable in the so-called Synoptic gospels—that is, in the gospels of Matthew, Mark and Luke—whereas the Greek faith-structure is dominant in the Pauline writings and in John's gospel. The line also runs, for that matter, right across the Jewish world at the beginning of our era. On the Jewish side there are authentic Pharisaism, Talmud and Midrash; on the Greek side we find the Hellenistic Judaism of the historiographer, Flavius Josephus, and the Alexandrian thinker, Philo the Jew, who is the impracticable "synthesis" of Greek philosophy and the Old Testament. Thus:

---

epistle to the Romans: "The righteous shall live by his faith" (Hab. 2, 4). Buber's translation has: "The proven one will live in his reliance" (*Werke* I:685). The great example of *Beharren* in *'emunah*, of persisting in trust, is Job (*Werke* I:679).

'èmunah	*pistis*
"authentic" Pharisaism	hellenistic Judaism
(Talmud and Midrash)	(Flavius Josephus, Philo the Jew)
Jesus	Hellenistic Christianity
(the Synoptic gospels)	(Paul, John)

Jesus therefore stands in the line of that whole world of faith which characterizes the Old Testament and prophecy in particular—a line which runs via Pharisaism at the beginning of our era on to Chassidism. Hellenistic Christianity does not stand in that line, and neither do Paul and John. Thus, anyone who wants to understand the significance of Jesus and his teaching—in particular, the Sermon on the Mount—in a proper light must first of all set aside his association with Christianity, which has made him into God. In other words, Buber sets out from the assumption that with the help of the New Testament text—and especially of the Synoptic gospels—it must be possible to penetrate "behind" the texts to the "real" Jesus. Buber believes in that possibility, unlike the majority of historians, the outcome of whose researches is either a verdict of "Ignoramus" or at the most a reconstructed picture, hemmed about with reservations of every kind (it may have been like this or like that). As a matter of fact, Buber's arguments serve to confirm rather than to confute their conclusion. It is clear, for instance, that when he comes to reconstruct the origins and growth of primitive Christianity, what he is really explicating are the presuppositions which as a Jew he has brought to his reading of the gospels. Apart from that, however, it must be said that Buber is much more circumspect in the way he sets to work than is the Jewish scholar, Joseph Klausner, who claims to know exactly what in the gospels is to be accepted as authentic and what is to be discarded as unauthentic, as well as how the "mists of dogma and mysticism" surrounding Jesus are to be dispelled.[4]

Jesus

Jesus, that great son of Israel, began his work with the proclamation: "The time is fulfilled, and the kingdom of God is at

[4] J. Klausner, *Jezus von Nazareth* (Jerusalem,[3] 1952) p. 168.

hand. Repent, and believe the Gospel" (Mk. 1, 15). Buber denies
that those last words are true. It was not to belief in his word, not
to belief in the Gospel, that Jesus summoned the Jews of his day,
but to *'èmunah*. Buber translates the text thus:

Erfüllt ist die gesetzte Zeit und	Fulfilled is the appointed time,
genaht die Königschaft Gottes.	and the kingship of God is
Kehret um und vertrauet. . . .	brought near. Turn about and
	trust. . . .

It is a call that combines three themes familiar in the Jewish
world: (1) the motif of God's kingship (cf. the study on the
theme of *Königtum Gottes,* in which the historical course of this
motif is followed through the Old Testament which has always
been there "in secret" and is now at hand; (2) the motif of the
teshuwah, which is to be conjoined with the first one, because *Königtum Gottes* only exists where people in fact apprehend it—
and that happens in the *teshuwah,* which is not an "interior"
event, but the turning of man to God with the whole of his
being; (3) the motif of the *'èmunah,* of unconditional trust,
which is something other than "believing that . . ."—for example,
that the man who speaks here is the *Mashiach.* What the saying
means is this: "The dynamism of the king of the world, always
and directly operative up to this moment but not yet visible as
such, in its movement from heaven to earth has now approached
so near that mankind, Israel, the Jew who is addressed in this
instance, may in the *teshuwah* grasp it as a lived reality" (*Werke*
I:667). This call which sounds throughout Galilee is linked in a
historical continuity with the proclamation of God's kingship—
for example, in the psalms with the call to "turn about" uttered
by the prophets of Israel, and with the call to *'èmunah.* The man
whose voice is heard here stands entirely within the Jewish
milieu. He stands out from it, but is still in his whole being a Jew,
just as the Pharisees are. The battle that he waged with the Pharisees—and the documented evidence is before us in the gospels—is
a battle fought within the frontiers of the Jewish world of faith
(*Werke* I:695). "It is clear, insofar as we are able to recover
(*erschliessen*) the real historical facts about him, that the religious sphere within which Jesus lived and moved was that of the
Talmud and Midrash" (*Werke* I:754).

Buber works this out in greater detail in an analysis of the Lord's Prayer (*Werke* I:768-69) and of the Sermon on the Mount (*Werke* I:690-708), an analysis which he takes as supporting his view that in their thinking about the Torah—a word that Buber would rather render as *Weisung, Anweisung, Belehrung* (instruction, directive, information) than as "law"—there is considerable agreement between Jesus and the Pharisees and a radical contrast between Jesus and Paul. Only on one point does Jesus go substantially further than the Pharisees—namely, in his injunction that we should not resist the evildoer (Mt. 5, 38) and that we should love our enemies: "Love your enemies and pray for those who persecute you, so that you may be children of your Father who is in heaven" (Mt. 5, 44f.; cf. *Werke* I:700-708). Even in this instance, however, the Jewish milieu is not abandoned, for Jesus' eschatological situation is different from that of the Pharisees. In other words, he is standing at the close of history, at the dawning of God's kingly rule (the *Königtum Gottes*), when what is "possible" is no longer to be taken into account; however, the Pharisees stand beneath the dominion of Rome within the ongoing course of history, in the *fortgesetzte geschichtliche Bereitung* (the continuing process of historical preparation) for the kingdom, and even in the teaching of the Torah they must have an eye to what is feasible. They cannot go as far as Jesus goes, whether they wished to do so or not.

That, then, is Jesus as he really was: a Jewish teacher at the very margin of time itself, the prophet of God's kingship, for whom the intention of the Torah was a matter of intense and unconditional concern, the man who was broken on a cross and did not rise from the dead: "The resurrection of a single man does not belong within the range of ideas (*Vorstellungskreis*) proper to the Jewish orbit of belief" (*Werke* I:746). What, then, has been done with him, and what has been made out of him?

At the close of St. John's gospel we read that Thomas had doubts about the resurrection of his Lord and that these were dispelled only when he had seen the marks of the nails in his Lord's hands and had touched them with his own. Then he cried: "My Kyrios (Lord) and my God!" (Jn. 20, 28), acknowledging that Jesus had risen from the dead, that he is his Kyrios and his God. "With that, for the Thomas of the story, the whole Jewish world of faith, which knows no God besides God, collapses at a single stroke. Among the disciples of Jesus he is the first Christian, as Christian dogma understands that term" (*Werke* I:747). For Buber the story is, of course, unhistorical, but it does show, with a clarity which leaves nothing to be desired, what took place soon after the crucifixion. Jesus is made into God, and at the same time *'èmunah* becomes *pistis*, becomes "believing that . . .": that Jesus is risen, that he is the Kyrios, that he is God, and so forth.

In this way there begins a process of "God-making", of divinizing, which is not capricious but rests on an intrinsic exigency (*Werke* I:748)—an exigency about which it is possible to say these things from a historical and a psychological standpoint, yet without rendering what occurred wholly transparent. Jesus did not intend matters to go as they did, and he set himself against it. To the man who addresses him as "Good Master" he replies: "Why do you call me good? No one is good but God alone" (Mk. 10, 18). Jesus is in line with the Old Testament, which is aware of the distance between God and man, but also of an immediacy in the relationship of man to God. It is as though he is here standing guard over the *'èmunah* against the divinizing that is looming ahead for him (*Werke* I:737), as though the Jew, whose living is rooted in the Jewish world of faith, is here throwing up his defenses against Christianity. It is the same in the nocturnal conversation with Nicodemus, recorded and preserved for us in the gospel according to John. "Here again Jesus speaks only as one who has faith, and not as a potential object of faith; in this place and in that . . . he sternly rejects the idea that we should turn him into the object of some belief" (*Werke* I:745).[5]

[5] This interpretation of the course taken by primitive Christianity recalls that of Karl Jaspers who, like Buber, took as his guides to the study of the New Testament Albert Schweitzer and Rudolf Bultmann, and besides them also Martin Dibelius. Jaspers is more convinced than Buber of the impossibility of getting behind the New Testament texts at the "real" Jesus. But for him too Jesus is a human being: a man of exceptional stature—and thus one of *die Massgebenden Menschen* ("the normative people")—but still a man. He was not God, but was *made* into God after his death by his disciples. "As long as Jesus lived the disciples believed with him in God, in his kingdom and in the end of the world. . . . After his death . . . [they] saw Jesus as the Risen One. Now they no longer believed with Jesus in God, but without Jesus in the risen Christ. That is the stride taken from the faith of the man Jesus . . . to Christianity." Cf. K. Jaspers, *Die grossen Philosophen* I (München, 1957), pp. 209-11. (= K.

Nevertheless he is made into God. Why? One reason, at any rate, is that the invisible, unknown, imageless God must acquire a face. In connection with the passage about Thomas, "the first Christian", Buber says: "For the 'Christian', as he is from now on, God has this face; but for this countenance he is what he was and is for the Jews: without a face" (*Werke* I:748). In the Jewish world of faith, of course, there are manifestations of God and, based on those, human ideas and conceptions too; yet in all his manifestations God has remained *unerscheinen* (without visage or outward appearance). "But now, in the context of Christian existence, the essential being of God can no longer subsist without a face. The Christian sees it directly as he turns to God. . . . Stephen, at the point of death (Acts 7, 59), commits his spirit not to God—as does Jesus at his own death (Lk. 23, 46; cf. Ps. 31, 6)—but to the Lord Jesus" (*Werke* I:748).

That is the end of *'èmunah*, the mark of which surely is that man's relationship to God is not only exclusive (*ausschliesslich*) but also immediate. This reality, experienced in faith and in life, a reality that has found its perfect expression in the daily summons "Hear, Israel. . . ." (Deut. 6, 4-5), is not shared by the Christian. In that quarter God is given a countenance: the countenance of "our great God and Savior" (Tit. 2, 13), of "the other God" (Justin), of "the suffering God" (Tatian), of the God "who has obtained his Church by his own blood" (Acts 20, 28).[6]

In this way, then, the Greek Gospel made its entry into the world, with the proclamation that Jesus is God and redeemer and mediator between God and men, without the *'èmunah* in which man relates himself to God exclusively and directly and believes as Jesus did. That is the start of Christianity: the raising of the

---

Jaspers, *Socrates, Boeddha, Confucius, Jezus* (Utrecht, 1960), pp. 147-49. It is worth noting that for a disavowal of the Christ-God Jaspers too appeals to Mark 10, 18; see K. Jaspers, *Der philosophische Glaube* (München, 1948), p. 76.

[6] The text of Acts 20:28 can be translated differently from the way that Buber has done it. Then it is a question of "the Church of God . . . which he obtained by the blood of his own (i.e., his own Son)". Thus reads the New Translation of the Nederlands Bijbelgenootshap, and the translation, issued in 1961, by the Katholieke Bijbelstichting Sint-Willibrord. In this translation God and "his own"—that is, Christ—are differentiated from each other. There is much to be said for this rendering, but of course Buber's outline of primitive Christianity does not fall down because of a single text in Acts.

man, Jesus of Nazareth, to the status of divinity, and the transition from faith in the Jewish sense to faith in the Greek sense of the term. Now let us return just once more to Jesus of Nazareth. Who was he?

Is the emergence of Christianity to be explained by the fact that he envisaged himself as the *Mashiach*, the Christ, so that there is at any rate a continuity between his self-understanding and Peter's words: "Thou art the Christ" (Mk. 8, 29)? In *die chassidische Botschaft*—a book which in its Hebrew version appeared in 1944, and therefore six years in advance of *Zwei Glaubensweisen*—Buber is positive about this. Jesus did regard himself as the *Mashiach*, and he said so publicly. He was the first in a series of *Meshichiem*, of "Christs", which ends with the "Christ" Sabbatai Zwi (1626-1675),[7] who set himself up as redeemer of Israel and of the world. "Whatever his appearance may signify for the *goyim* . . . viewed from the Jewish standpoint he was the first of a succession of people who laid claim to messianic status and broke faith with the secreted character of the servants of God, the real 'messianic secret' " (*Werke* I:755). This is not to say that Buber classed Jesus with the fanatic Sabbatai Zwi and the other "Christs" of Jewish history. Jesus was the greatest of the line, the most pure, and more than any of the others was endowed with real messianic power. All the same, this whole movement was a *Fehlgeschehen*, an aberration.

The aberration was not that Jesus knew himself to be possessed of messianic power, but that he arrogated to himself the status of being *the* Christ. *Everything* that people do in God's name is a messianic activity, but truly messianic behavior can only happen without premeditation or design and without stopping to dwell on one's own messianic function. Even for the person who participates in the messianic activity, the "messianic secret" remains a secret. Such is the sense of the introduction to *Die chassidische Botschaft*. Six years later Buber was somewhat more cautious, although what he had to say about the self-understanding of Jesus (*Werke* I:726-736) went pretty far in the same direction.

[7] On Sabbatai Zwi and on the apocalyptical movement which he and his prophet, Nathan of Gaza, stirred up during the years 1665-1666, cf. Josef Kastein, *Sabbatai Zewi, der Messias von Ismir* (Berlin, 1930), and Gershom Scholem, *Die jüdische Mystik in ihren Hauptströmungen* (Zurich, 1957), pp. 315-55.

But though there may be an aberration here, Jesus was nonetheless a servant of God. What Buber means by that becomes
clear if we look up the texts of the anonymous prophet who lived
during the 6th century before Christ and is known as Deutero-
Isaiah, the second Isaiah. Among those texts are what are called
the songs of the servant of Yahweh (Is. 42, 1-7; 49, 1-7; 50, 4-11;
52, 13—53, 12). The songs speak of a man upon whom God has
laid his Spirit. He will not shout and raise his voice in the street;
he will establish and restore Israel and at the same time he will be
a light for the *goyim;* in lowly service he will take it upon himself to suffer and so will accomplish the work of Yahweh upon
the earth. "In my view the life history of Jesus is not to be
understood unless we realize that he stood within the shadow of
the servant of Yahweh in Deutero-Isaiah (as Christian theolo-
gians, especially Albert Schweitzer, have also pointed out). But
he left the concealment of the quiver (Is. 49, 2), while the 'holy
Jew' remained within it" (*Werke* III:1260). What Buber has in
mind in the final words of this passage is the strange utterance of
the servant of Yahweh: "He made of me a pointed arrow; in his
quiver he stuffed me away" (Is. 49, 2)—which is as much as to
say that concealment or secrecy is of the essence of the servant's
being. He is *"der Pfeil, der sich ins Dunkel duckt"* ("the arrow
that bends in the dark") (*Werke* III:1261). Presently he will be
discharged and will find his target, but not yet. For the present he
goes quietly on his way, taking upon him the suffering which is
part and parcel of the messianic role.

For Buber this servant of Yahweh is not one man but a recurrent figure, present ever and again in this guise and in that. The
6th-century prophet whose very name is unknown to us was the
servant of Yahweh, and so was Jesus, and so were the *tsaddikim*
of the Chassidic world. The servant is in "the line of servants of
God, who . . . though humble and despised, bear the infirmities of
the world and purify them" (*Werke* III:754). They are the
harbingers of the end, of *die endzeitliche Messianität* (the ultimate messianic condition), which in their hidden activity is of
every day and age, and amid them the world that has fallen away
from God could not subsist. But what is essential is their *hiddenness,* in which their true identity is unknown even to themselves.

"The messianic mystery stands or falls by its secrecy; not by a kind of secretiveness, but by a real, factual hiddenness, reaching into the peculiar depths of the mystery itself. The people through whom it makes its way are those of whom the nameless prophet says that God makes of them a 'naked arrow' which he then tucks away within his quiver. This hiddenness of theirs pertains essentially to their role of suffering. Each and any of them could be the man to accomplish all, but none of them may be to himself anything more than a servant of God. If the hiddenness, the incognito, is shattered, it is not simply that the work comes to a halt; a counteraction begins. To announce one's own messiahship is to break connection with the messianic quality of being" (*Werke* III:755).

Jesus was one of the people in whom the servant of Yahweh makes his way through the world—but Jesus broke through the limits of hiddenness. He was one of the greatest men in Israel's history—so much so that he is not to be contained within the usual categories—but he negated his messianic status because he was aware of himself as the Christ. Although that was an aberration, he remains one of the great sons of the people. The break with Judaism comes not with him but with Paul, who made the man who suffers for the work of Yahweh into the God who suffers for the sake of men (*Werke* I:763). From that moment on, the paths of Judaism and Christianity separated.

Judaism and Christianity

Is it possible for them to meet again and to become one? It is unlikely. The fact is that they are essentially different, and these differences do not relate to small matters but reach to the inmost character and core of the two religions. Judaism and Christianity, in their deepest essence, are mutually *alien*, and thus it will always be "until humanity is brought home from the exile of the 'religions' in the *Königtum Gottes*" (*Werke* I:782). Meanwhile, that is not quite the last thing there is to be said on this point. "An Israel aspiring to renewal of her faith and a Christendom striving for the renewal of hers should have much to say to each other which has not so far been said, and they could offer to help each other in a fashion which at present we are scarcely able to conceive" (*Werke* I:782). That is why so much depends on the encounter between Judaism and Christianity, on the study of the New Testament by Israel and on the study of the "Old Testament" by Christendom.

The Unity of Buber's Work

From all that has been said we might gather the impression that Buber occupied himself with many things that are admittedly important, but still are divorced from real life. The study of the faith of Israel, of themes like the *Königtum Gottes*, the translation of the Old Testament, the study of Chassidism, the meditations upon *Gottesfinsternis* and the analysis of the contrast between the Jewish *'ĕmunah* and Christian faith—what has all that to do with the genuine issues of our time? Such questions may perhaps spring from an overhasty and self-confident assumption that we know what are the "genuine" issues of "real" life, but they give us occasion to pause for a moment at the end of this book and to consider the unity of Buber's work.

When Heidegger was asked in 1946 what sort of meaning may still be attached to the word "humanism", he replied in a letter to Jean Beaufret: ["Humanism is] taking thought and care that man be human and not inhuman, or 'out of character'."[1] I believe that these words not only express the major theme of Heidegger's writings—which means that Heidegger is not the nihilist he is often said to be—but that Buber, if asked what it was that most concerned him, could reply in the same vein. What matters is that man in the 20th century—marked as it is by such great and rapid changes—shall be "human", shall take hold of the possibilities afforded him and shall put them into effect. Buber's concern, in other words, is with the building up of a truly human society within which man, in close alliance with the eternal Thou, encounters the people around him not as an It to be used and manipulated, but as those with whom he *lives*.

In a capitalist society such a thing is impossible. Buber had early found his way to socialism, and in the religious socialism that followed World War I he played a major role. He was in

[1] M. Heidegger, *Platons Lehre von der Wahrheit mit einem Brief über den "Humanismus"* (Bern, 1947), p. 61.

full agreement with the Marxist critique of the capitalist system, as uttered by Karl Marx in the Communist Manifesto: "Where the bourgeoisie have taken power into their hands, they have done away with all patriarchal, idyllic relationships. . . . They have left nothing between man and man but naked self-interest." Thus states the Communist Manifesto. In Martin Buber's language, the system has put an end to all traditional forms of community and has deposited man in an overwhelmingly functional and matter-of-fact It-world. "The bourgeoisie have dissolved the value-status of the person in market-value," says the Communist Manifesto. Buber comments: "When we inquire regarding the character of the capitalist society in which socialism has originated, we see that it is structurally deficient (*strukturarm*) and will become more so" (*Werke* I:850). To get a clear view of what is being said here we have to know what Buber means by "structure". He defines structure as *Gemeinschaftshaltigheit* (a firm principle of common interest or partnership). Capitalist society is deficient in structure—in other words, it is deficient in genuine community, and therefore in genuine humanity, and that is not some fortuitous and avoidable deviation, but is given with the system and is an inescapable consequence of it.

Humanism, therefore, means socialism, and socialism means restructuring society, creating room for those "idyllic relations" (to use Karl Marx's expression) which the market economy of the 19th century negated and which will be still further disrupted. Here, then, lies the very core of Buber's thought, and his study of the Old Testament and of Chassidism, his theology and his anthropology, are not to be dissociated from this major theme, this crimson thread running through his life's work—the restructuring of human society, the "structure" of which has been lost. Humanism means socialism. Socialism means restructuring. Socialism in Buber's sense is something different from Marxism.

Netiwot-be-Utopia is the title of a book that came out in 1947 in Tel Aviv. *Pfade in Utopia* (*Paths to Utopia*) is the title of the German translation, published in 1950. The book has also been translated into English, Spanish, Japanese and Yiddish, but not so far into Dutch. There is a reason to suspect that it was written much earlier, for the most recent literature mentioned by Buber in the book dates from 1933. In any case, the "restructuring" motif—even if not referred to by that name—is much earlier than *Netiwot-be-Utopia*.

Utopia is the name for a world that does not and cannot exist, that has "no place". Thus Thomas More set down his Utopia in writing: the design of a perfectly human society. But Buber did not settle himself to the task of describing a fantasy world and the way that might lead to it. His title bears on one of the chapters of the Communist Manifesto, the program of the League of Communists, written by Karl Marx and brought out in the year of revolution, 1848.

The Manifesto starts off with an exposition of the class struggle, which has now reached its final phase, with an exposé of Diamat and dialectical materialism, and with a series of demands. Then comes some critical comment on "socialistic and communistic literature", which is not conspicuous for its sticking to the point or for any desire to accommodate the others, so far as might be possible—but the Manifesto is, after all, a polemical document, even in this direction. Thus Marx disposes of reactionary socialism, of conservative socialism—he mentions Proudhon and his *Philosophie de la Misère*—and of the critico-utopian socialism that he finds in the French socialists St. Simon and Fourier and in the Scottish manufacturer, Robert Owen. Their systems, too, are pulled to pieces and dismissed, although this part of the Manifesto is written with a measure of sympathy. They had at least been revolutionary, but they built castles in the air, and their puny experiments, doomed to failure, produced no results.

It was from this section of the Communist Manifesto that Buber borrowed the title of his book, *Netiwot-be-Utopia*, a socialist and anti-communist Manifesto. Buber ranges himself against Marx and Marxism and on the side of the "utopians", of Saint-Simon, Fourier and Proudhon, of Kropotkin and Gustav Landauer, of those who seek for ways to restructure human society from the bottom up, on a basis of small communities, *associations fraternelles* (Proudhon).

There are two types of socialism, therefore: there is a line running from Karl Marx via Lenin and Stalin to Moscow and on to the "world revolution", and there is another that begins with the French socialists and leads to Jerusalem and the kibbutzim. Both are forms of a secularized eschatology, but whereas Marxism is an implementation of apocalyptical eschatology, "genuine" socialism is an extension of Old Testament prophecy. Here the choice lies.

"Inasmuch as Russia has not herself undergone a fundamental, inward change—and we cannot at this moment guess when and how that will happen—we are obliged to denote one of the two poles of socialism between which we have to choose, with the mighty name of Moscow. I venture, despite everything, to refer to the other pole as Jerusalem" (*Werke* I:992). Moscow or Jerusalem! *Netiwot-be-Utopia* appeared before the death of Stalin, and during the Khrushchev regime certain changes did take place. There can be no doubt, nevertheless, that the choice is a real one. Moscow or Jerusalem: the bureaucratically governed and uniform Soviet state, or the *communitas communitatum*, the community (federation) of communities, which it is Israel's business to be.

Our concern in this book is not with the history of socialism but with the work of Martin Buber. The question, therefore, is not whether *Netiwot-be-Utopia* gives us an historically correct outline of the thinking of Karl Marx or of Proudhon, his greatest opponent, and of the course of the Russian revolution—it strikes me that Buber was rather inclined to schematize everything—but what, for Buber, is the "genuine" socialism which is lacking in the Soviet Union and has taken shape, albeit in a provisional and very imperfect form, in the kibbutz.

The problem is to introduce structure into a world that has become structurally deficient, to set up community in a world that is geared to *Gesellschaft* (organized, functional relations).[2]

---

[2] It would appear from the text of *Netiwot-be-Utopia* that in his use of the term "community" Buber has in mind, for example, the book—one that has gradually become out of date—by the German sociologist, Ferdinand Tönnies, *Gemeinschaft und Gesellschaft*. In this book, which dates from 1887, the word "community" (*Gemeinschaft*) connotes "being bound up by destiny together", which is abstracted from my own choice. In *Gesellschaft*, on the other hand, it is precisely this "destined solidarity" that is lacking; relations are established and broken again, and all these relations have an end in view, are "in aid of" something or other. In community it is possible for love to exist—and if love is absent, then the "community" has already to a large extent disappeared; in *Gesellschaft* people find themselves in the milieu of right and duty: duty which is

State socialism contributes nothing to the restructuring of human society. If something is to happen, then it must be achieved in small communities of people who are really and truly living together in *associations fraternelles*, to use Proudhon's phrase. What man does not bring about himself, with his own will and his own being, whatever else it may be, is not restructuring. In other words, the socialist vision and the profoundest longings of mankind acquire a palpable form not in the monolithic State in which everything is controlled from the top—not in the state of Israel, either—but in a federation of small-scale living communities (concretely, in the Palestinian "community-village", the village commune, the kibbutz).

However, the mere fact that here and there settlements spring up which are real communes does not take us very far. It is neither here nor there that by communal effort a strip of desert is brought under cultivation, and that because of this a small number of people are able to affirm and consolidate a "truly human" existence. That is good in itself, but it is not enough. In the first place, there must come some form of federal association between these communes which will encroach as little as possible upon the autonomy of the constituent *communitates* and on their freedom to seek after a form of their own; secondly, the ambiance of the kibbutz must extend to urban society so that there too a new *communitas*, a mode of living together that is truly human, may be built up. And even that is not all. Assuming that in Palestine— the year is in fact 1947, and so we are still talking in terms of Palestine—a new national community is taking shape, its credentials must be such that in the world of the *goyim*, which has come to be so deficient in "structure", people will feel it to be a real way out of the dilemma of a collectivism which annuls all freedom and an individualism which destroys all solidarity and mutual connection between men. Shall not the Torah—as the ancient vision has it—go forth from Zion and the Word of Yahweh from Jerusalem (Is. 2, 3)? That the Arab population for that very reason must form a part of the national community in process of emerging in Palestine is so obvious in this line of

---

done, right which is maintained. These two structures of human society tally up to a point, though not entirely, with Buber's fundamental paired terms, constitutive of a world and of man within that world: *Ich-Du* and *Ich-Es*.

thinking that Buber was not disposed to reckon with any other possibility.

It is clear—and here the great unity of Martin Buber's work is for all to see—that this *communitas communitatum* can *only* be established on the basis of the *teshuwah*, the turning of a man with his whole being to God and to his fellowmen, and on the basis of the Chassidic dream of the *yichud*, the task of unification which God has entrusted to man; it is also clear that the first thing necessary here is the *tsedākā*, the strength to stand firm and to persevere in that simple confidence in which man is for God and for his fellowmen.

So much for the vision, the "logical" rounding off of what we have heard so far. And the reality? In the course of writing *Netiwot-be-Utopia* Buber sees that only to a small degree has the experiment succeeded. Many of the illusions of the *chaluzim*, the pioneers, have been destroyed. The despair that was bound to follow is one which is no longer felt, but it is retained in the work. Anyone who takes a complete and realistic view of the matter must conclude that it has not gone *totally* awry, that there has by no means been a complete miscarriage, and that, keeping in view the history of all socialistic experiments, this *Nicht-Scheitern* even has an exemplary value. The way is open; the work continues. Such is the state of affairs in 1947.

And in 1968? In the meantime the State of Israel has come into existence, and its achievements have been considerable. Has a new *communitas* emerged as well, or is the State of Israel, with an energy that cannot but command our profound admiration, in the process of developing into a modern State on the Western model and as structurally deficient as the latter? Has the dream of the *chaluzim* not gone up in smoke? Do they still stand in line with a utopian socialism, rich in faith, reaching out heroically toward the heights? Does the mysticism of the messianic spirit live on in the new Israel, or is this perhaps the final question:

The tried and trusty one—what may he do? (Ps. 11).